1 Billion 800 Million
Christians

MISS HEAVEN!

FREDERICK SMITH

Copyright © 2018 by Frederick Smith.

ISBN Softcover   978-1-951469-29-0
      eBook   978-1-949723-68-7

All rights reserved. No part of this book may be reproduced or transmitted in any form or by any means, electronic or mechanical, including photocopying, recording, or by any information storage and retrieval system without express written permission from the author, except in the case of brief quotations embodied in critical reviews and certain other non-commercial uses permitted by copyright law.

Printed in the United States of America.

To order additional copies of this book, contact:
Bookwhip
1-855-339-3589
www.bookwhip.com

Where does that leave YOU??

Remember there is a New Earth. But NO one seems to know who goes there and WHY? They all just assume they're going to Heaven and Pastors just let them believe it. Why?

This 1 billion 800 million number comes from Revelation 9:13-18 about the number of the army of <u>*the Horseman! I explained*</u> in my last book "They Have Revelation Absolutely Wrong". More is explained in this book. John 12:48; "The words "I" speak, shall Judge you". Why take chances? Re-check while there's still time.

PREFACE

If Christians don't take the time to recheck the scriptures on a subject like this they are making the biggest gamble on their eternal life EVER! Jesus made numerous warnings about false Preachers and those who follow them. "If the blind lead the blind BOTH fall into the ditch" [of hell]. Jesus also said; "Because you are Lukewarm I will spit you OUT My mouth"; He didn't say you were UNSAVED, just lukewarm meaning average, mediocre, casual etc.]. Also did you notice all He showed that were CAST back, cast down, told to depart, and bind him were all SERVANTS of His, and IN His house and field. Also did you notice every time Jesus mentions Heaven He ADDS something like; Sells all; Forsakes all; does not love even family more; and Bears Cross [ready to DIE for]?

If there is only one Holy Spirit and He tells ALL one truth why are there so many different Denominations? If Jesus says; "My sheep hear MY voice…'; "strangers they will NOT follow…". Why do all in these Denominations think they will be forgiven if theirs is wrong? When He says; "Many false prophets SHALL come and Deceive MANY…'" why would a person deceived get the reward of Heaven? Remember His sheep hear His voice!!

We are told to take His massage to all, or at least those in our circle. The more we witness to the more our reward. Daniel 12:3 "….and they that turn MANY to righteousness shall shine s the brightness of the firmament and as the STARS forever". Notice the many. John 15:8 "Herein is the Father glorified; that ye bear MUCH fruit". It's all about the maximum not the minimum!! If Jesus was down here now He would do the same thing He did before. The footwork of Preaching and spreading the WORD. Christians are always praying for Jesus to save people. He's gone and left the work to His faithful [FEW] who will do it even with our busy schedules. He said; "Pray the Father send workers into His vineyard". Why do we have to pray for that? Because the laborers are FEW". He KNEW most of His born again baptized believer's won't do anything but the minimum of His work and the maximum of their OWN earthly material gaining work. John 15:2 "... Every branch IN Me that bears not fruit My Father takes AWAY". If Christians will not double check their beliefs HOW can they witness to Muslins, Buddhists, and Hindu's and tell them to RE check their beliefs?

In this book we will examine about 20 scripture Topic's with additional scriptures on that subject to RE check if we are going to Heaven. Because remember there is also a New Earth. And it's for ALL those who refuse to Re check, and are following "commandments of men" not the voice of Jesus Christ.

One last thought. Have you EVER heard preached in your church that just like your name goes IN the Book of Life; it can come OUT the Book of life?? Revelation 3:4-5. If not ask yourself WHY your Pastors are withholding that kind of information? They won't tell you, but "I" will. I pray this book doesn't bore you because SCRIPTURES should NEVER bore a Christian.

TABLE OF CONTENTS

Chapter 1. "Willful Sin" 1
    Hebrews 10:26-29

Chapter 2. "Fear" 5
    2 Thess. 2:3"

Chapter 3. "False Prophets" 9
    Matthew 7:15

Chapter 4. "Denying the Power" 13
    2 Timothy 3:5

Chapter 5. "Bundles & Clusters" 16
    Matthew 13:30 & Rev. 14:18

Chapter 6. "6 Servants Fired" 20

Chapter 7. "The Laborers" 24
    Matthew 20:1-16

Chapter 8. "Deny Himself" 28
    Matthew 16:24

Chapter 9. "A Proud Look" 32
    Prov. 6:17 & Luke 14:11

Chapter 10. "Adultery & Fornication" 36
    Galatians 5:19

Chapter 11. "Judge Not" 40
    Matthew 7:1-5

Chapter 12. "Thinks No Evil"... 44
    1 Corinthians 13:5

Chapter 13. "Examine Yourselves"...48
    2 Corinthians 13:5

Chapter 14. "Stars Fall From Heaven"..54
    Matthew 24:29

Chapter 15. "Worship in Vain"...58
    Matthew 15:8-9

Chapter 16. "I Never Knew You"...63
    Matthew 7:23

Chapter 17. "Weeping & Gnashing of Teeth"......................................67
    Matthew 25:30

Chapter 18. "Fire Not Quenched"...69
    Mark 9:46

Chapter 19. "Beaten Many Stripes"...71
    Luke 12:47

Chapter 20. "Forsake All"..75
    Luke 14:33

Chapter 21. "More Than Conquerors"...79
    Romans 8:37

Chapter 22. "Victories in Poetry"..83

Chapter 23. "This Isn't New"..86

CHAPTER 1

"WILLFUL SIN"

"If we sin willfully"; Hebrews 10:26-29

Each chapter will list a scripture topic that will absolutely keep person out of Heaven. We don't have to look hard to see numerous Christians' sin just like the unsaved. Even Pastors, and it's all over the news. By doing this we put our Lord Jesus "to and open shame". It's not just US we show as weak. We are giving ammunition to the world that Christianity does NOT work and they use it to say we are ALL hypocrites. How dare a believer think they will be forgiven! It even says in verse 27 "..There remains NO more sacrifice for sins".

If we examine Isaiah chapter 5 we see a story of God and His vineyard. He says he did everything for IT. Cleared the rocks, watered, fenced it and it STILL brought forth WILD Grapes! Or the same as the world with No one attending to it. He says; "YOU judge" this? "What MORE could HE have done". He goes on to say "He will tear it down and destroy it". Don't say this is just the Old Testament because Jesus did the SAME for the New Testament people AND gave His Own life and Holy Spirit. And yet look at the churches today. People see them the same as the world.

Don't they chase the almighty dollar like the unsaved? Don't they cuss like a drunken sailor if they get mad like the unsaved? If a man or woman is cute enough don't they fornicate and commit adultery like the unsaved? Don't they side with their relatives even when they SIN?

Jesus said plainly do NOT love anyone more than Him? Remember the Prophet Eli in first Kings did that, and what happened to him.

When Jesus says in Matthew 11; "…learn of [from] Me" why do Christians rely totally on their pastors with their eternal future? He says the Holy Spirit will be in us ALL and Teach us all. [1 John 2:27] The problem with not having time to study OR say we don't understand it well enough is that we become WEAK. So weak we will not be able to endure the last days, or much of any conflict that comes.

These pastors will never tell you about the Great trials we are about to see. Matthew 7:24-27 Jesus speaks of when "storm and wind and rain and flood came and BEAT upon that house it FELL…and GREAT was the fall of it". We are that house. The one that fell did not DO what Christ said, but what he thought He said. Because he put his faith in the Pastor without checking. The house that didn't fall was as Jesus said; he that hears these sayings of MINE and doeth THEM are built upon a ROCK' and does NOT fall. Remember also about the Broad and narrow ways in verses 13-14 of chapter 7. Verse 15 tells why the road is so BROAD going to destruction? "Beware of false prophets"!!! If you are fooled it is your OWN fault, for Jesus said; "His yoke is easy", and "My sheep hear My voice". If it was impossible to hear Him we would not be at fault.

No one can use the excuse of it was too hard either because 1 Cor. 10:13 tells us; "There is no temptation on us but such as is common to man…God will give us a way of escape that we may bear it". This does not mean we will never ever sin. It means IF we do it, they are far and FEW between. And when we do we are greatly sorrowful for them and repent very quickly. We do not do like David when he sinned with Bathsheba. It took a prophet to come to David a year later and confront him before he admitted it. And he was greatly punished. David did what we should never do; he STARED too long. Or dwelt on her nakedness too long. When we happen to see something like that or anything that entices us we should turn away quickly before the evil thoughts take hold and cause and ACTION by us.

Our topic is "sin willfully". But what is SIN? Most can't even answer that without a long drawn out answer. It is simple. 1 John 3:4 "....sin IS transgression of the LAW". Or the breaking of the 10 Commandments. Many go months without lying, stealing, killing, adultery etc. But churches today say "no one's perfect" and "we're all sinners". This gives leeway for many to do these and think its ok. These 10 are things Paul says in 1 Cor. 5-6 we are put a person OUT the church for doing. It is not ok. Ephesians 5:3; "let it not ONCE be named among you as becometh saints". So we always set our goal to never brake the 10. If we do get weak which does happen we repent right away. But we don't keep doing it period. Remember "greater is He in us than he that is in the world". We make Christ look weak and He will not be mocked.

We all should study Romans 14. It tells us the difference between things we do NOT judge, like 1 Cor. 5-6 showed us things we DO judge. Notice nothing in Romans 14 is a 10 commandment! They are all small mistakes Christians make because they don't have enough knowledge and faith YET. But we should be careful not to push these things as LAW in the churches because we happen not to do them. I personally don't drink because God told ME not to drink. But I know drinking is not a sin for others, but IS for me. Smoking cigarettes, Saturday worship, drinking etc we never go beyond the Bible. I won't go much into how we are "not under the law" anymore and cannot be charged with sin anyway. I will say we will not be charged with the SIN but DISOBEDIENCE to Christ!!! We are under Grace by obeying Him.

For very mature Christians I tell this: sin is the least of a true Christians problems. No real Christian will break the 10 anyway. Jesus took care of the SIN on the Cross anyway. He knows we are weak. He does ask us to do something. Take this massage to the world, or at least everyone in our circle. We don't have to be a preacher to witness to neighbors and friends. Fear keeps us from that. Our sin is gone and "remembered no more". He just asks us to WORK. Not to be saved but because we are SAVED.

I have told 2-3 lies in 18 years and repented. Lies can jump out our mouth so fast to protect our egos. I have said 2-3 cuss words in 18 years. No other violations of the 10 in 16 years. "we are MORE than conquerors". You can do this also.

So we see this chapter on sinning willfully. This will absolutely keep you out of HEAVEN. You will be rejected at the Judgment Seat of Christ!!

CHAPTER 2

"FEAR"

"Falling away first" 2 Thess. 2:3"

We see already churches are not nearly as full as they used to be. Our children don't have the same fervor for God like we had. We see sin running amuck even in the churches. If you witness much, you will hear many tell us "they used to be in the church and saved and deacons etc". We see many money grabbing pastors, and fornication by church leaders which discouraged many and they left the church. But what they really left was God Himself. Jesus said "he that endures to the END shall be saved". Yet these who left still think God will reward them for time they did do good. Ezekiel 3:21 tells us; "… the righteousness he has done will NOT be remembered". And Hebrews 11:38 Jesus says; "..if any fall back My soul shall have NO pleasure in him". No pleasure at all period. It doesn't sound like any forgiveness is coming.

This falling away in 2 Thess. is Not the great falling away Paul is speaking of, but we get to that later. The question is why Christians are so weak to be falling like dominoes? There are several verses on this starting with the 2nd seed in the parable of the sower. "He received the word with JOY…but when persecution and tribulation came he falls away". Why? One is he had no root or faith that comes from studying the Bible. Most Christians leave the study up to the Pastors. It is them who need the strength. Study "IS" what gives us "the whole amour of GOD". But worse is if you can spiritually see it, is this man was surprised that ANY trouble ever even came!! He was NOT told that by the preachers. Pastors don't want to discourage anyone so they leave OUT this most important part. All they want is to keep the seats and offering plates FULL.

Look at the many scriptures on persecution of Christians. "all who will live right Shall suffer persecution". "..Offences will come but woe to him that causes the offences". ".. ye shall have tribulation 10 days". These are just a few. Now look at what will happen to these one side preaching Pastors. Ezekiel 3:21; "if you fail not to warn them their blood I will require at YOUR hand". Romans 20:26-27; "I am free from the blood of all men because I failed NOT to give you ALL the counsel of God". It is the Leaders who will pay dearly for holding back the bad parts that Christians need so they can prepare for what's coming.

This is why the beast is described in such terrible language like; "7 heads and 10 horns and mouth like a lion, feet like a bear etc." And in Daniel 7; ".. Dreadful, terrible, devours, breaks in pieces, and stamps the residue under his feet". This is for us to get ready for the most horrible thing possible. If we over prepare we can handle it with faith to spare. "We are more than conquerors". Jesus said He gives us power to "tread on snakes and scorpions; and over ALL the power of the enemy".

This Holy Spirit in us is the same as was in Jesus. And look what happened when it descended on Jesus at baptism. It says; "Immediately He was lead of the Spirit into the wilderness to be tempted of the devil". Who was picking the fight with the devil? The Holy Spirit!! Evil is NO match for what we have in us. This is why there will be NO excuse for us. By falling away and getting scared, we make God look weak to the world. Revelation 21:8 those that went to the Lake of Fire, starts with: "..The FEARFUL". Before it mentions any sinner.

"Who shall separate us from the love of Christ"? Tribulation, life death etc". In "all these we are more the conquerors". Rev 12:11 "...they loved not their lives unto the death". "He that will seek to save his life SHALL lose it". If the devil can scare you with death you may as well stop now. He will get most with just money and their material things because they will lose it all that like Job did anyway; when the mark law comes in. Some will fall for sex. Some just because "they loved darkness [sin] rather than light".

So we see that unless we study to build our faith up now, before this terrible beast comes we are in trouble of falling. Your pastor can not stand for you. Each of us must have the faith to stand alone with by the Spirit. God set it up this way to separate the wheat from the tares. The sheep from the goats. The lukewarm from those on fire for Him. Christians will be wishing hard God would come before it gets real bad but He won't. 1 Cor. 3:13 "the fire will test every man's work". The fire is the 1st Tribulation. There are 2 parts. The 1st is bad but not nearly like the 2nd. When we are raptured out before the 2nd and Great Trib. Starts, NO one will be left alive! "He who seeks to save his life Shall lose it". 2 Thess. 5 tells us; "quench not the Spirit". The Holy Spirit can defeat the enemy. We in our humanness cannot.

Then we have Hebrews 11:37-38 about those from the Old Testament who before they saw the promise, were tortured in many horrible ways. The Bible says; "The world was not even worthy to have these people among them". We see in Rev. 6:9-11 those that were "slain" and given white robes. Romans 8:18; "the sufferings of our present time is not worthy to be compared to the glory…" 1 Cor. 2:9; "eye has not seen nor ear heard the things which God has prepared for those who love Him". My goodness; look at the promises made to us by God. And can we say we don't see His presence all around us every day? I often compare humans as goldfish in a bowl in your living room. They see many things around that room they can NOT begin to explain. What they are for, or what they made of. And WE sit here on earth and see all the things in space we cannot explain. But at least we have an explanation of some kind that there's a GOD. Any explanation is better than none. Evolution just doesn't cut it for me!

Fear hit those all through history and in Jesus time. The story of the blind man is not just about him being healed. It's about the PRESURE put on him and his parents for believing in Jesus. It says it right there in John chapter 9. They were put OUT the church for not rejecting that miracle. John 12:42-43 those went along with the crowd because; "they loved the praise of men more the praise of God". Many today will not go against the crowd and norm and friends etc. Jesus tells us in Luke 14:28; "which of you intending to build a TOWER sits not down first and counts the cost". He means a tower too! If you are going to heaven you will stand out far and above the lukewarm Christians. We are called His ELECT! Cream of the crop. Picked over and CHOSEN.

Well we see a 2nd thing that will surely keep us OUT of heaven. There's more. But we are more than able with HIM. He just says trust Him. We have power to "trample on snakes and scorpions, and over all the power of the enemy".

CHAPTER 3

"FALSE PROPHETS"

"Beware of False Prophets" Matthew 7:15

This title really starts at verse 3, about the Narrow and Broad roads. Jesus tells us that FEW are on the narrow road and MANY on the broad road that leads to destruction! Many means MOST in most of Jesus teachings. He wants us by the Spirit to seek the answer of WHY? Very few Christians have time to investigate any of the mysteries. We are too busy with the "cares of this world" and our OWN agenda's. But let's figure this out now. Why are so many being fooled? Both of these roads say they lead to heaven. The answer is in the very next verse. Verse 15 says; "beware of false Preachers". Yes appear to be the real thing, but they are NOT. He says; "you will know them by their FRUIT". The problem is Christians who weren't very serious when they accepted Jesus, don't study their Bible to learn what teachings are true or false. Their fruit is what they teach and how they live.

There are many stories showing false Preachers all over the Bible. We will look at just one for now in John chapter 10:12-13 He calls them HIRLINGS. Or a person who is PAID to do the job. He cares not for the SHEEP but the money! Without the money he would not even be doing the job Pastor and Teacher. When the enemy and trouble come they FLEE. Peter says: "they make merchandise" out the churchgoers. Or use them for the money. Yes a certain portion of money is given to supply the Preachers NEEDS; not extravagance. Paul said in 1 Cor. 9

he would not accept money for Preaching so no one could say he did it for money at all.

Look at the churches today and how rich the Leaders are? Even a small church provides a very nice living for the Pastor. They still teach TITHES which went out with the Old Testament. Now we "give as we purposed in our hearts; not grudgingly or out of NECESSITY" 2 Cor. 9:7. We must realize back then the 12 were taught by Jesus. In Acts when they sold their things and laid the money at the Apostles FEET, those 11 knew better than take it and use it on high priced material things. They would never do what these do today with Gods money.

But it goes much farther in Matthew 15 they were changing many of Gods Laws with their own Traditions of the Elders. Look at the denominations today and how each teach their own traditions. They are either right or wrong period. Yet they insist on making them mandatory for their members. Some are not a threat to your going to heaven. Romans 14 Paul tells of several things Christians do that we LEAVE alone. Such as drinking; things we consider holy days, and eating certain foods etc. But some he slams as wrong such as tongues. To hold something as coming from Christ and it does NOT, is to blaspheme Christ period. "Oh foolish Galatians, who has bewitched you". What saved you is what will keep you. The Galatians changed and started believing something else had power also to get them to heaven. Paul said you can NOT have both.

I was a junkie, alcoholic, criminal, mental patient 31 years and God changed me in 1 day! As soon as Jesus did His work here come the professional Christians telling me; "what God did was good, now let ME tell you how it goes". Why would I change for them when they could not deliver me for all those 31 years in sin? I was in their churches, 10 drug programs etc. Now they want to fine tune me. I and we all need to know it is the WORD that saved us, not any church. Once we are saved we need to follow that WORD, not that church! But it's hard to go against a whole church and pastor. Or is it? I did and so did many others. We are PURE at salvation but when we start following the Traditions of the particular churches we immediately become defiled!

That's what the Galatians did. That's why Paul had to keep writing the Churches he started and visited to make sure false teachings hadn't slipped in and defiled them. He knew the devil would slip in and change things even just a little. Even a little change in Jesus truths can make you MISS Heaven and Paul knew that. Guess who else knows that? The DEVIL! He knows God will not let them in Heaven and he will laugh as they are cast BACK to earth from the clouds at the Rapture.

Most never heard that when we are Raptured up, we have a stop to make BEFORE Heaven. It is the "Judgment Seat of Christ"! That's where we will be separated as sheep and goats; and wheat and tares. If we obeyed Christ OR Traditions of the churches. Revelation 14:18-19 the angel with power over fire [in charge of the great tribulation the devil] is the saying to the angel up in the clouds with Jesus who also has the "sharp sickle"; "gather the clusters of the vine of the earth and cast them {back down to the] into the wine press of the wrath". The devil knows Christ will NOT take you into heaven if you believed FALSE teachings. Because He says; "MY sheep hear MY voice, and strangers they will NOT follow". You don't deserve to be in the same place if you were TRICKED by the enemy; and your Pastors!

Remember Jesus said of "outer darkness… there will be weeping and gnashing of teeth". The weeping is from getting their feelings devastated. Imagine you worked 40 years for something then get to pay day and find out it was all wrong! That's what happen in Matthew 7:22-27. "We prophesied in your name; cast out devils; did MANY wonderful works" [according to who? Not Jesus]. Jesus says to them **"depart I never knew you".** Can you feel the utter horror they will feel? Many things that LOOK Christian are NOT. Verse 24 explains why. "He that hears these words of MINE, and does THEM; is like a man who builds on a ROCK". He does not fall in the Great Trib. But the one who builds on sand {traditions and denominations} is NOT doing what Jesus SAID. He is NOT hearing Christ's voice! Please compare these in Matthew 7 to the ones who DID get IN, in Matthew 25. "Come ye blessed of My Father"… "When I was hungry, thirsty, naked, in prison" etc. you came to me". Notice the difference in their works? One did the nice easy cleans jobs, the other worked with the POOR. One did show off jobs, the other dealt with people churches don't want to deal with. Which did Jesus deal with?

See how many are deceived? Revelation 7:9-17; "GREAT multitude no man could count". Yes they had white robes, but **NOT linen** robes like those in Heaven in Rev. 19. Notice they had "**palm branches**" not **HARPS**" like the ones ON the "sea of glass" in Rev. 15:2. All this has BEEN in the Bible for years, yet our Pastors did not interpret them right, IF they bothered at all. Most of this wasn't meant to come out till now anyway. But if Pastors don't know them they should NOT ever preach guesses! Isaiah 5:14; "therefore hell has ENLARGED herself, and opened her mouth without measure". God saw He was going to need more room for some of His own people to go there. That chapter talks about His vineyard and how much He did for it, yet it brought forth "wild grapes" [just like the world]. Can you ignore this STILL?

<u>**Remember John 10:5, 27;**</u>
<u>**"Strangers they will NOT follow" at all period!**</u>

CHAPTER 4

"DENYING THE POWER"

2 Timothy 3:5

When we look at each chapter we will always make sure it's in context with the verse mentioned. We see the first 4 verses 3:1-4 deal with horrible personality traits. Paul says how CHRISTIANS will be in these last days. Not just the unsaved! Church goers have tendency to put everything on the unsaved. But here Paul IS speaking of Christians, because he says they; "have a FORM of Godliness; but DENY the Power". What Power of GOD are they denying? The power to CHANGE their horrible personality traits. We see in all churches people with tempers and attitudes that come out at the drop of a hat. Most are still selfish like sinners. "Lovers of their OWN selves". Not homosexual; they love them some THEM! They never "denied themselves". We can't do Christ's will if we are doing our OWN thing.

We see many other traits in Christians here that are not Christian. Let's take a few. 1 Cor. 13 tells us of TRUE Christian LOVE that the Holy Spirit is supposed to put IN us. It is "LONG suffering; does behave unseemingly; endures all things" etc. If a Christian goes off on a cussing temper tantrum or fight; or is selfish etc., he is DENYING God has the power to STOP that in him. Most just call it their personality and excuse it. It will now be excused at Judgment. 1 Cor. 5-6 Paul tells us "put people OUT the Church if they are a railer, disrupter etc.

How can Christians have a temper like the unsaved? "Let your speech be always with Grace, seasoned with salt". No hurtful, unkind words should come out your mouth. Remember how they knew Peter was a follower of Jesus? "Your speech betrays you". He didn't talk like the rest of the people. Our words say a LOT about us wherever we go. Our GOD does have the Power to change our hearts. Our speech comes from our hearts. "Out of the abundance of the HEART the mouth speaks". "Every idle word shall be brought into Judgment". If we can't control our tongue, we are not letting the power of the Holy Spirit do His job of being Head in our life. Oh yes it's our fault. 1 Thess. 5; "quench not the Spirit". It is US who stops the Spirit and deny God His power in us. Which makes not only US but GOD and Christ look weak. He isn't having it at Judgment. We put Him; "to an open Shame". The world looks at us and says; "that's why I don't go to church; they do the SAME as we do"!

The fruit of the Spirit is; "Love, Joy and Peace". If that is IN you it should SHOW to all you meet. If Jesus could heal a man possessed with many demons, who broke chains; He can fix our horrible Personality traits. Remember we represent CHRIST on this earth. All who see us are supposed to see Christ in us. Christian means Christ LIKE. Shame Him and you will NOT enter Heaven period. Don't chance this, you will get your feeling hurt at Judgment.

Read all 15 or so horrible personality traits and let's check ourselves with them. Boasters & proud? Do we do this? Proverbs 6 says; "6 things GOD hates". Number one is not murder, it's "a proud look". Whether it's because of our money, race, car or clothes etc. If we have pride in our hearts He HATES it. "Without natural affection"? Do we need something to stimulate Holy affections? All with these personality traits will MISS Heaven.

"Truce Breakers". Look how many Christians do not even keep their word. They lie like the world. There was a time when a person said they were a Christian it meant something! Now when you say you are Christian people think a CON game is coming. And many times it is. All over the news we see Church People even Leaders being guilty of horrible crimes. They didn't just not keep their word to humans and the laws of the land, they broke their agreement with Jesus Christ who they said they would obey! "Be ye not deceived, God is Not mocked; whatsoever a man sowed that shall he also reap".

"Despisers of them that ARE good". Have thought if Christians are willfully disobedient, or just weak? They do not want to see anyone else following Gods word? It has gotten so bad most think it's Ok to mess up constantly and call it normal. They say; even Preachers; "We all sin; nobody's perfect etc." I plead with you don't go to Judgment with that thinking. I wish Christians could understand 1 John 3:6, 9. About how sin works; "we SIN NOT; and can NOT sin". I don't have time to explain how sin works for Christians. Romans 8:1 "we are not condemned". At Judgment Christ will decided if we are charged, or not charged. Not with SIN, but disobedience to HIM! Hebrews 10:26-29 tells us "if we sin willfully there remains no more sacrifice for sin". His blood was shed to be for our penalty for sin, but it will NOT apply. That is a hard statement in verse 27; "There remains no more sacrifice for sin".

No one can accuse us of anything. It is Christ who died and will decided if our sins are covered, or IMPUTED [we are charged]. If we do His will to our best [and He knows what our best is] we have nothing to worry about. I often say; "sin is the least of a REAL Christians worry". Because a real Christian is NOT going to sin if at all possible. Romans 12:18; "IF it be possible; with ALL that lieth in you...." Sometimes it's not possible! But we feel horrible and repent right away. If you deny God His power to change your un Christian ways you will absolutely miss Heaven.

I will leave you with this to study and think on. 1 John 3:4; "Sin IS transgression of the LAW". But Romans 6 – 7 says; WE Christians "are NOT under the Law". You'd be surprised how many are playing God for an all-day sucker, because the Pastors said we are forgiven and guaranteed Heaven. Don't bet on that. There's a great penalty. After that penalty there is the New Earth. But you will MISS Heaven.

CHAPTER 5

"BUNDLES & CLUSTERS"

Matthew 13:30 & Rev. 14:18

We have here a verse all have read yet never saw the importance of the word BUNDLES. In many of Jesus parables there are key words that need extra attention to understand. They can only be found by the leading of the Spirit. You cannot learn them from human bible schools and colleges. If it was so you would have heard the pastors and scholars preach on them before. So let's see what the Bundles mean completely.

First off why are they being GROUPED in Bundles? What groups are being separated in and why? These same bundles are the CLUSTERS in Rev. 14:18 called the "Clusters of the Vine of the EARTH". Jesus is the TRUE vine so these must be Religions of the earth. Or to put it simpler, all those cast out and rejected by Jesus at the "Judgment Seat of Christ". Yes they accepted Christ and were baptized, and scripture says; "he that believeth and is baptized SHALL be saved". So yes they are IN Christ. Now remember Rev. 3:16 Jesus says of the Lukewarm; "I will spit you OUT My mouth". He didn't say they were NOT saved, just that they were average, mediocre, and casual. But yet saved but were following a false form of Gospel from false Preachers.

The parable in Matthew 13:24-30 & 36-43 about the "Wheat and Tares". Jesus does say the world is the field. But He says HE has a field also IN this world. When He came He cut out a portion of earth as "HIS FIELD". So we read the keepers or Leaders of His field realized there were Tares in His Wheat field. Jesus said: "an enemy has done this" [devil]. He said; "don't you try to separate them or you may root up some of the wrong plants". The Reapers will do the separating at the end; or Judgment Seat of Christ. The explanation in verses 36-43 we see it's the Angels who reap and separate the TRUE from the False, **while [IN THE AIR CLOUDS]!**

There is something else very important the Leaders MISS. Why is the devil putting ANYONE in Jesus field when he wants all unsaved; and evil to destroy them? Remember He said "an enemy has done this". If the Pastors never preached on this they never saw it by the Spirit period! Well here it is. All want to go to Heaven and none to hell. The devil knows that many will go to churches and seek heaven anyway. So he comes up with a plan to FOOL them that they ARE going to Heaven, when he KNOWS they'll be rejected at Christ's Judgment Seat. This is the Narrow and Broad roads of Matthew 7:13-14 & 22-23; those who did many wonderful works and prophesied. 2 Cor. 11:13-15 "false leaders and satan transformed into ministers of Christ". Jesus says; "leave tares alone". They can't harm the wheat anyway. Matt. 24:24; "If it were possible they would deceive the very ELECT". You can't fool a REAL Christian!

All these the devil set up with a false doctrine, taught by a false preacher, in a false church or denomination. The devil KNOWS Christ will not accept them into heaven. Now I must say they can get eternal LIFE but not in Heaven but on the New Earth! But here's the advantage the devil has going for himself. He gets a second chance to get them forever. When they are rejected and cast BACK from the Rapture as Unworthy to earth the Beast & False Prophet & Devil are in Charge down here and the Holy Spirit has left. The door to Heaven is SHUT [Rev. 6:14 & Matt. 25:10. So NO prayers can even get through to Heaven during this time.

The Cast Back can get the New Earth but ONLY if they STILL; "keep the commandments of God" when cast back Rev. 12:17. The devil and Beast will KILL them all. They MUST die to show their Faith. "He that will seek to save his life SHALL lose it". Even before the Rapture when things are already bad for Christians many will hide to save their life. But after they are cast back the only way to get the eternal life on the New Earth is to let satan KILL them while still living Christian. After being up there & seeing Christ, and what is POSSIBLE most will be ready to let the Beast do to what he will to them because had a TASTE of the eternal and Glory. Can you imagine being down here with the billions who have NO chance at salvation and those cast back still do? Not just the Beast but all the humans will be extremely mad and violent to them because you still have a chance. OH; maybe you thought they can still be saved like the Preachers say: "tribulation Saints". NO; those Saint who came out of Great Trib. In Rev. 7:14 ARE those CAST BACK who were saved BEFORE the Rapture! Remember we are "saved by FAITH". When the world sees the Rapture there is NO more Faith involved because they SAW God is Real. No faith, no salvation period.

Now let's get the part of WHY they are bound in Bundles and Clusters? You can even use your common human sense on this one. What groups would they be grouped with? The same groups they CHOSE down here on Earth. The same groups they had Faith in down here. What groups do Christians put their Faith in? Denominations! Remember there is only one Church and it is a Spiritual Church and BODY. The TRUE VINE who hear Jesus Voice. So if there are 200 different Christian denominations all teaching something different then 199 or all 200 are NOT hearing Christ voice. He said "STRANGERS they will NOT follow"! We have tendency to pick out the worse as we see it like the JHW, Catholic's and Mormons. But that would still leave 196. So let me just tell you they are being bound *by their denominations they trusted in. Bind all the Baptist, Methodist, Tongue Speakers, JHW, Evangelical's etc. etc. in separate Bundles Or Clusters and CAST them "into wine press of the wrath of GOD" [Rev. 14:19].*

Another very important proof of this in Rev. 14:16-19. Its Jesus WHO used His Sharp sickle to REAP [bring IN]. Then ANOTHER angel comes from the Temple where the Father is and has also a sharp SICKLE. He is told to **CAST** [from UP there], not bring IN like

Christ did. Remember Jesus said; John 15:2; "every branch in ME that bears not fruit My Father CASTS away. Well that's what that angel from the Temple is doing on the Fathers orders. One last thing is it mentions and "angel with power over FIRE" [authority over the Great Trib.] That IS the devil who is NOW on Earth [Rev. 12:12-13]. "And he knows he has but a short time" [before he goes to the lake of Fire].

Jesus knows who His are. We can go to ANY Church but we KNOW Christ & our Faith is NOT in a Church. We will SPEAK up and say so whenever possible and if asked. We are not there to disrupt the church but we MUST speak the truth. Jesus said of REAL Christians; "They will put you OUT the churches". I been put out of about 9. How many have you been put out? Or do you feel security with the crowd? If you are in the majority, you are in the WRONG! "FEW find LIFE"! Our comfort comes from the Holy Spirit, not the majority or the Church. Our Faith is **in CHRIST ALONE.**

CHAPTER 6

"6 SERVANTS FIRED"

What we will see in this chapter is ALL these were IN Christ. That's why they are called servants, or as we say today Christians! Christians seem to think we are shoe-ins, and have it made. The church leaders let us think that and seem to back it back it up with scriptures such as; "We are SEALED with the Holy Spirit". Yes we are sealed but for only ONE reason and it's in Romans 8:11; "The same Spirit that raised up Jesus will quicken our mortal bodies". That means yes the Holy Spirit MUST raise us up at the first resurrection. Rev. 20:5 says; "But the rest of the dead lived not". Only those who were saved have the Spirit to raise them. The unsaved don't have Him. So they don't get up till the 2nd Res. John 5 says the same; "The hour when ALL that are in the graves shall hear His voice and come forth". That's the 2nd Res. We must know there are 2 resurrections and 2 Judgments. One for the saved and one for the unsaved.

We will look at several Jesus called Servants as He fired, rejected, and told them to depart. That means they were IN Christ. The first is the Lazy Servant in Matt. 25. He was IN the master's house and a worker. He was given a JOB like an employee. When Jesus returned he said he had HID the master's money and not even used it. He was cast OUT. Now let's see why; in way you may have never heard. The master was gone a LONG time. He WAS doing something in all that time. Whatever he was doing it was not the Lords business, but his OWN thing. He used that time for his own gain and pleasure. It says Jesus gave them; "according to their ability". Jesus knows our abilities. He gave the one guy only 1. You can't give less than 1, and didn't even use the 1! We need to see ourselves today as that Lazy servant. How many of us are doing our OWN thing and not Christ's WORK? When we go to Judgment many Christians will say how they paid off their house, put kids through college etc. but He will say to you; "you miss understand Me. What did you do for the Kingdom's sake; My work not your work? We are supposed to be about His business, and fishers of men. Most don't have time for His work because we have our lives too wrapped up in our own agenda's. He was kicked out and fired and so will we be.

Let's look at the man with no: "Wedding Garment" in Matt. 22. The question is HOW did he get up to where the wedding was going to take place anyway? He got there because he was a servant also down here. No sinner will get there period. What he didn't know was and we don't know is before the wedding there is a STOP to make in the clouds as we saw in Rev. 14:16-19. There we are judged or CHECKED to see if we are worthy to be IN the wedding to Christ. That's Christ's Judgment Seat. That's where all mislead and bad Christians are CAST BACK from. So what does the no wed garment mean? He thought he WAS dressed right. He must have had on his best clothes. That's why it says; "He was speechless". He was clothed in his OWN Righteousness. He did what he thought was right and would get him in. He did not follow Jesus words but what he thought and heard from whoever. Look how many today still go on what they think and feel. They swear God should be a certain way. We MUST never under mind John 12:48; "The words "I" speak SHALL judge you". He got fired and kicked out also.

Matt. 7:22-23 tells of those who said; "We prophesied in your name, and cast out devils, and did many wonderful works". Yet He says; "Depart from Me, I never knew you". They were also servants because they were doing the Lords work a long time and thought it was right. Can you imagine the utter devastation they felt for doing something 20-40 years and find out it was NOT right? A total let down! What can be wrong with what they were doing most ask? Let's not say they had secret sins in their life. Let's give them the benefit of the doubt on that. But a key to the answer is in verses 24-27 of Matt. 7. "He who hears these sayings of MINE and does THEM". They obviously were hearing what someone else said that seemed good and did THAT instead of reading and checking the Bible. I always say compare these to the ones who DID get IN in Matt. 25; "Come ye blessed of My Father". Notice the difference in their works. One did the show off clean jobs, the other worked with the POOR, hungry, sick, imprisoned etc. Churches today don't even want these around. They were Fired and kicked out also.

Let's look at the 4 seeds in Matt. 13 about the Sower. 4 seeds and the first did nothing with the Word so we leave him out. But the next 3 did. The $2^{nd;}$ "Received the word with JOY". Yet when Tribulation came he falls away. But he did receive it, so he was saved! Fear caused him to fall, but why? He must not have heard the part about "we shall suffer persecution and tribulation". Preachers today only tell the easy and good parts. Telling only the easy parts will get these Pastors sent to the Lake of Fire. If they cause their whole congregation to miss heaven and suffer the Great Trib. They deserve the Lake; 1 Cor. 3:17; God says. They won't even get the New Earth. But his falling away gets him FIRED.

The 3rd seed also received the word but was TOO busy and occupied with other thing's [mainly making money] he bared NO Fruit. This IS the lazy servant we saw in Matt. 25 who hid the Lords money and did his own thing all that time the Lord was gone. In today's society and tech age we are super swamped with things to do. We can't find time for Jesus work. We'd rather just give money and let someone else do it. That's why the scripture says; "The cares of this world"; and "The lusts of others things". There some swamped with other things that don't involve riches. Things like sports, video games, hobbies of all kinds that take up our TIME and none of this involves Jesus work.

When Jesus was down here He did the footwork preaching the Gospel. Now that He's gone He told US to do it. "As the Father sent ME so send I you". Christians pray; "Lord saved these people". We are asking Him to come back and do what we won't do! He's not coming back to do it. He said; "Pray the Father send laborers into the vineyard".

The laborers are FEW because we are too wrapped up in our own lives. We did not: "Deny ourselves". He is not number one in our life, we are. The 4th seed; Understood IT". What did he understand? That he had to DO something, and did bear fruit.

John 15:2; "Every branch IN Me that bears not fruit My Father takes away". Notice the branch is IN Christ but will be taken OUT and Fired. All this time we are in churches Jesus hopes we will finally SEE these things because at Judgment time is up. No excuses, we failed and will be FIRED. Christians; SEE the truth before it's too late. Christians can be FIRED!

Every time Jesus mentions Heaven He adds something like; forsakes all. Sells all. Loves not his life unto death etc. Jesus knows humans are lazy and lie. They talk a good game but won't DO anything outside their comfort zone. You will not receive the same reward as those who DO the right work and deny their comforts. We are on a JOB, and we supposed to WORK!

CHAPTER 7

"THE LABORERS"

Matthew 20:1-16

This parable must be broken down so we don't miss the Spiritual point. This also shows a group NOT making Heaven. In all parables there are key words that if we miss them we miss the whole insight of the parable. This one leaves us with a mystery of why these FIRST hired were called out LAST to be paid. It's important because so many Christians think they do not have to do anything once saved but stay away from sin, or just praise and worship. There is a reason they want to see it that way. They are lazy or scared, period! Coupled with that you have the Pastors telling them it's DONE at salvation. We must consider John 15:2 "Every branch in Me that bears not fruit My Father takes away".

In this parable we see the owner needs to hire workers and they agree to a penny a day. The penny represents eternal life. As the day goes on the owner comes back 4 more times and hires more and more to work. And the last set He hires said "They didn't even know there was work in the vineyard" [because the first ones never told anyone]. Remember Christian's job IS to tell all about this owner Christ and the job to get the work done. Getting the work done is the goal. Remember "The harvest is plentiful but the laborers are FEW". Our job is "Fishers of men". There's enough work for all who come plus more.

As we read more we see the owner comes back to pay the workers. But He says; "Call the LAST hired OUT of the vineyard to be paid

FIRST". Leaving the others IN there working. Why is this; IS the question. It seems only fair that those who worked longer would get paid first or at the same time. So what can be the reason? I haven't ran across anyone with the answer yet that I have. We know our Lord is fair and judges rightly, so there must be a good reason.

I say it's because the first hired were NOT working! They were lollygagging on the job. How can I prove this? First the owner knows how long and how many it takes to pick a vineyard. He's been doing it for years. He hired enough IF they had been actually doing the work. It was their job to get more help, not the owners. If you still don't see it remember; "Pray the Lord of the harvest send workers into the vineyard". Jesus knew of all those who say they believe in Him MOST were NOT going to do anything!

Look at the churchgoers today. They go to church and BACK home. People can know them for years and one day say; "I never you were a Christian". Some don't act like Christians in public and on their jobs anyway. We are supposed to; "Let our light so shine". "No man lights a candle and puts it under a bed". We are supposed to be a TOWER that no one can miss anywhere in the area. Now most Christians think their lives do show Christ, but I tell you it doesn't.

Does it go even further than just what our life shows? Do we have to speak UP about this? John 7:7 "The world cannot hate you but Me it hates, I testify [speak up] of it, that deeds are evil". Jesus is saying of real Christians we MUST speak up! And only we who speak up will understand the scriptures anyway to put conviction on the hearers. John 7:17 "He that will DO the will of the Father SHALL know of the doctrine". God is not giving His mysteries to people to just keep it to themselves! No one lets people know their inner most secrets unless they are very close to them. That's why in Matt. 13:11 Jesus says; "It is given to YOU [the 12] to know the mysteries of the Kingdom, but unto them it is NOT given".

Only Christians who DO the will and obey the commandments will get more insights. If we have willful sin, or are following false teachings we will not know the truth. We will only know what our particular denomination tells us. It takes TIME out of our lives to do His work. Time most of us will not give up. Most don't even realize we are still on a JOB. Pay day has not come yet. "Every branch that bears fruit My Father purges [prunes] it that it bear MORE fruit". The Father will cut even more out of our lives so we will have time to do more. It's about the maximum not the minimum. Daniel 12:3; "......They that turn MANY to righteousness shall shine as the stars forever". What's the opposite of this? If we don't we will not shine as a star or Spirit being. Meaning we will not be in Heaven. Those on the new Earth will be in a new human body, not a spiritual one like those in Heaven. John 15:8; "Herein is the Father glorified; that you bear MUCH fruit". There again it's the maximum we are called to do.

Going back to the parable we see if the LAST hired are OUT of the vineyard where are the first? Still in it, and it represents the Earth. We are paid in the clouds away from the earth. What is going on, on the earth? Those who came later said they; "Bore the BURDEN and HEAT of the day". This is the Great Tribulation they had to endure. All go into the first part of the Trib. But at the Rapture those who worked get out and go into Heaven. Revelation 15:2 they are standing on the Sea of Glass in Heaven. I pray you can see this now. Yes the others complained but they got their PENNY; or eternal life. But LATER and not in Heaven.

Christians don't get it yet that we are saved from the WRATH of God which is the 7 plagues of Rev. If we do what He said, and not our denomination. "He that believeth shall not perish" and is not [condemned]. Both these mean the Lake of FIRE you will not go to. All can go to Heaven if we get the Gospel right. "My sheep hear My voice".

I want to show one more short story Jesus gives about Heaven. Every time He mentions Heaven He ADDS something. Matthew 13:44; a man finds treasure in a field and hides it. So the treasure is secure and is eternal life. Jesus says that ISN"T enough for a real Christian. This man "Sells all he has and buys the whole field". He wants more and knows there's more treasure in that field. He's not lazy and will dig, search, pull weeds, rocks and whatever to get more. The average Christian will be satisfied with just the eternal life because that's all the Preacher said is needed. Average is lukewarm. Lukewarm gets "Spit out". He's coming for His elect [best] on the first round. Those who proved while down here by their lives that they truly loved Him. "If you love me keep My commandments".

The last verse in this 16; "The last shall be first and the first last". Many career Christians will be left to the 2nd Res. Jesus will call people from the "highways and hedges, streets and lanes, poor maimed and halt to do the work career Christians SHOULD have been doing all this time. Matt. 21:31; "Sinners and Harlots go into heaven before YOU". This chapter shows another set that will not make Heaven. If we get our eternal life on earth or in Heaven is up to US. You don't have to be one now that you know this.

CHAPTER 8

"DENY HIMSELF"

Matthew 16:24

Here is another scripture most Christians do not apply nor understand. They purposely refuse to examine it because it will interfere with their own TIME in life. When Adam sinned he and all after him were born thinking of self to the extreme. Selfishness rules in us from birth. We have the "me and mine syndrome". Yes we are to take care of our families and ourselves but there is a way to do it without letting others be in suffering. Jesus showed us how He could live and **GIVE** and not worry about tomorrow at all. It is a part of our Faith in God and His promise to provide for our needs. Matthew 6 covers this in detail. 4 times it says; "Take no thought for our life what we eat or drink or clothes". This is madness to non-Christians and even Christians today. They do not apply this scripture to see if it works. Malachi 3:10-11 God says; "Prove [test] Me now". And He will rebuke the devourer for our sakes. God loves those who trust Him. We do not have to chase the dollar, riches and security like the unsaved. We will find out we even have enough to give the poor. We have security.

Believe me I have tried Him and He does not fail us. James 4:3 tells us we pray or ask; "amiss, that we may consume it of our own lusts". Even the prayers we pray are for selfish things to show off with like the unsaved. We are promised food clothes and shelter. Not steak lobster tailor made clothes and mansions. Christians should not even have it in their mind to want these things like the unsaved. 1 John 2:15-17; "Love not the world nor the things IN the world". Christians cannot see these as doing any harm when it surely does. Our minds are supposed to be: "Set on things above not on things of the Earth". Jesus warned His 12 many times about this kind of thinking and they obeyed it even after He left. Remember when they brought the money and laid it at their feet in Acts 4:35-37? They knew better than take it and live high class lives. But today these Pastors live like kings with Gods money. 1 Timothy 6:8; "With food and clothes let us be therewith content".

Now we must be reasonable in all things even this. If a person has a good job and makes good money honest money he can easily afford better things than most of us. And there's no problem with that, and we poorer should not have an ounce of jealousy toward them. The problem comes when we STRIVE to get these things causing strife and stress in our life. Sure we do make life as comfortable as can for ourselves and families. But with the Holy Spirit guiding us we KNOW what is overboard and what is not. No one can make that limit for you. Jesus will judge what was sin your heart at Judgment. You can fool humans but not Him. But many things are so obvious even to humans. When a person wants a luxury car, shoes, clothes it shows where his heart is. With the material NOT the Spiritual! So did that person EVER really deny himself? It takes TIME to do Gods work down here. The reason most can't do His work is they are using their time to get these material things as the scripture says. The seed among thorns; "The cares of this world and deceitfulness of **riches choke** the WORD {off and OUT} and he becomes UN fruitful". We go to hell for being UN fruitful with Gods work.

Some look at the extreme and say crazy things about our need for free time and relaxation. Yes; yes we do need time to wind down. Jesus did it a lot. He had to take His 12 out to the mountains and private places a lot to relax. We can relax doing things we like, like a hobby, games, fishing, vacations, etc. god knows our human bodies must get a break from every work. "The Spirit is willing but the flesh is weak". Yes we are called to do His work and He knows the personal limitations of each of us. He will judge us according to what our personal abilities were. But we have tendency to claim weakness where there is none. In the army they say give me 50 pushups and you say no, I can only do 10. Believe me you will do the 50 if it takes all day. Humans have the ingrown need to find an easier way, or get out of work altogether. We cannot fool GOD! We will miss Heaven!

Now let's look at other ways we do not deny ourselves. We have goals in life we want to accomplish. We set our sights on homes and where we will live. How much it will take for our new cars, children, retirement etc. we have our whole lives planned out THEN we find Christ! Now we read we need to deny ourselves. The best example I can give is that of John the Baptist. First do we really care what Jesus and Heaven thinks of us? Do we love the praise of God more than the praise of MEN? Well Jesus said of John; "There is none born of women that is greater than John the Baptist". Why did He say that? John had a one track mind period. He came eating locust and wild honey dressed in camel hair in the desert. This is Gods PERFECT for Christian humans. To just have a one track mind. Our main goal in life is for Him and His work. Yes we have other things to do, but our minds are never off His work. When something is in our spirit and mind we can access and enjoy it 24-7. "In that law does he meditate day and night". Yes He will show us where the line is for us and His work. It is different for us all. Some have more natural abilities, some less. Not I nor anyone can tell you to what extent you should be witnessing. But believe me don't try to fool God. You'll miss Heaven.

But yes we DO put our plans aside for our earthly goals because now we have a heavenly goal. We now; "lay up treasure in Heaven" NOT on earth. "We see ourselves [now] as strangers and pilgrims on this earth". We now serve 1 master, not the mammon master. Christians try to get all the money they can, but only all the God they NEED to make Heaven. God will not be equal with anything or anyone in our life.

Lastly look at our love for family. Luke 14:26-35 tells us all about where family is supposed to stand when it comes to God. God knows we love them and He commands us to love and take care of them. But there again is a limit. We let no one come before His will and work.

Matthew 12:46-50 the Pharisees wanted Jesus to stop Preaching and couldn't. When they saw His mother and brothers they told Jesus: "Your family are standing outside wanting to SPEAK with you". Jesus did not stop. He said; "See these [listening to Him] standing HERE; he that does My Father's will the same IS My mother, brother and sister". The devil will use our UN saved family every time he can IF it will work. We will find ourselves missing church etc. because of family. Satan uses anything and anyone we love to deter us from Gods work. We MUST decide we if we love GOD more than family because it WILL come up.

    I have NO goals in life but to do His will. Yes I take time off to relax but I have nothing in life I'm trying to accomplish. Can God brag on you like He did JOB and John the Baptist? He can we truly DENIED ourselves [within reason]. If we haven't yet; do it. Or we will MISS Heaven.

CHAPTER 9

"A PROUD LOOK"

Prov. 6:17 & Luke 14:11

The proud look title comes from the Old Testament; but we are not under the LAW anymore. So I will use the same topic but is in Jesus words from Luke 14:11; "He that exalts himself shall be abased". We will show several ways this proud look can come out even in people who don't yet see it. Yes some really do not see this PRIDE when it comes. This will definitely keep us out of Heaven. This is what the devil let get control him as we will see. I have seen it rise up in me, but recognized it. Proverbs 6:16-18 tells of 6 thing's God HATES. The first is not murder, nor the second. Here they are in order. Verse 17; "A proud look; a lying tongue; hands that shed innocent blood". Murder is 3rd on God's list of things He hates. We that are spiritual can see how pride can and does lead to murder.

So why is pride so evil and dangerous? God made all things and humans. He knows what we are made of, and that we are inferior even to the angels. Isaiah 2:22; "Cease from man whose LIFE is in his nostrils [breathing]". Heavenly beings know all humans can die in an instant real easy. Only the eternal carries any real weight to eternal beings. Luke 20:35-36 Jesus tells us that those who make Heaven will be "equal to the angels and can NEVER perish". Showing us even all the angels are eternal. Yes God will destroy them meaning quarantine them in the Lake of Fire. Isaiah 57:15;"He [GOD] inhabits eternity". When you have ALL power and everything was created by you, you don't need to explain yourself to any lessor beings. When God sees a human swell up with pride it just gets His goat. How dare one inferior being say to another inferior being; "I'm better than YOU". We are all dust, and come from one blood.

Let's look at some ways this pride may come out. Money can easily make a person's head swell with pride even without knowing it right away. If I buy a Rolls-Royce and drive it; my nose will go up a little higher whether I know it or not. My millions will put me above so many others I will FEEL like I'm better than they are. 1 Timothy 6 warns of the hidden snares of riches. Even a pair of 200.00 + tennis shoes can; and all expensive clothes puts a person's pride level on automatic rise. If we have a natural ability at something pride can go up. And now a days the MOST common form of pride that the devil slipped in people is the pride a RACE and color. Hitler didn't start it but he perfected it beyond anyone in history. His main hatred was for the Jews. The Jews had gotten the bighead and thought God would not punish them because they had HIS Temple and Abraham as their father. God let the Temple be destroyed and them taken into bondage. Let me say something about people who say God must be prejudice because He picked the Jews. No it wasn't like that. He knew he would NEED a place for Jesus to be born into that KNEW about Him, and He had stopped dealing with humans directly after Adam sinned. Plus anyone on Earth could come in and join the Jewish Faith. God said if they did they would be: "As one BORN in the land". No discrimination could be brought against them at all. And remember even Moses married an Ethiopian wife and his sister and Aaron complained about that and were punished. Oh it goes even further.

Jesus saw how the Pharisees were full of pride, and the rich also. He warned His 12 they would NOT be like them. Mark 9:35 Jesus tells the 12 [when who shall be the greatest came up] "He who is the greatest among THEM shall be the SERVANT of all". It is supposed the opposite in Christianity. The 12 had that pride rise up in them even having Jesus with them. Matthew 23:5-12 Jesus gives several more warnings about pride and ways to stop it from coming in. He said; "Call no man father........we are ALL brethren [even Preachers] and are to be called brothers" [and sisters]. So where did the name reverend come in? The bible says; "Reverend and Holy is HIS [Gods] name". Yet Preachers love to be called that. Also in Matt. 23 warned about wearing the ROBES. Those also make a person's pride go up. Yet we see the church leaders LOVE those long ROBES. The outward appearance has even Christians fooled. They see Pastors as MORE than Jesus wants them to be seen. They are stealing the focus from the Lord, and His Glory also. I will show you something from my last book on Revelation. The 2 Witnesses that will be preaching shortly are warned in Rev. 19:10 & 22:8 not let humans worship THEM. "I fell down to worship at the ANGELS feet". This is not in here by accident. John IS one of the 2 Witnesses. And when he comes back and people KNOW he walked and talked with Jesus and the miracles he will DO himself; they WILL literally try and worship John. They fell down before Paul in Acts. John is warned do NOT let that happen. We need to be on guard for pride.

People's egos today even has the poor filled with pride when they get anything better than the next poor person. Schools are all about clothes and shoes etc. There are now millions of millionaires that a million is nothing today. Now they seek the billion mark. The billionaires seek even more. No one satisfied. Proverbs says; "He that loves silver shall not be satisfied with silver" [or anything]. "All is vanity and vexation of spirit". We chase the wind and it's useless. All Christian's need to be on the lookout for this because the devil slips it in many of their spirits in the churches. James speaks of a man coming in church with ragged clothes and one with fine clothes and a gold ring and where they seat them". Luke 14 Jesus tells the story of a man giving a party. "Do not invite your rich friends who can pay you back; but the poor who can't pay back and you will have treasure in Heaven". But what is more important to most? The pride of being around the rich and famous! Romans 12:16; "Mind not high things but associate with men of low estate".

God resists the proud. He has chosen the poor rich in Spirit. Jesus was called a FRIEND of sinners. Somehow Christians today think they're too good to go around sinners. We don't do as they do. We are there to witness to them like Jesus did. 90% of Gods work is not in the church but in the FIELD! We are like 1st century church who kept hanging around Jerusalem after the Holy Spirit came. God set a situation where Paul came and started persecuting and killing them and they spread abroad to get away from it. This is what God wanted in the first place; His Word SPREAD to all the world. Christians today are still hanging around Jerusalem [church].

Jesus said he that does not receive the kingdom as a little CHILD, shall not enter in. There is no pride in a child. Pride rose up in the devil; "I will be like the most high". We are to deny ourselves once we become saved. Remember God hates pride worse than MURDER. How dare we rise up like we something better than the next human! The devil uses RACE and skin color today in a BIG way with millions being lost. Jesus will not let you in Heaven with that in you. You'll suffer a WORSE punishment than death in the Great Trib. [Hebrews 10:29].

CHAPTER 10

"ADULTERY & FORNICATION"

Galatians 5:19

This is a subject that should not even have to be written. What Christian doesn't know that ANY sex out of wedlock is a sin that will definitely keep us out of Heaven? Many today just assume God will excuse this especially if they only do it every now and then. We will examine this by all the scriptures concerning this. First every time the Bible lists a list of sins it starts with Adultery Fornication. It's because the first thing the devil will tempt us with is the "Lust of the flesh". Yes all humans have a NEED for sexual satisfaction. And the Bible gives us a way to do this. We MUST marry, period! God made us with different standards than animals to be with only one partner for life. There is NO side excuse that the Bible gives at all. If we do it we are guilty period. Yet today Christians have watered down that law to make a way for modern norms and our young people who see this as outdated.

Let's first see that it will not and cannot be excused. Ephesians 5:3 about fornication; "Let it not ONCE be named among you" [not even once]. So when we hear people say "We all sin"; or "nobody's perfect"; or "I'm a man and God understands". None of these will hold water at the Judgment Seat of Christ". It has gotten to the point if a Christian says their getting married a year later; no one wonders if or why they can abstain from sex that long? Even if they are getting married it still doesn't give them a free pass to break the Law of Fornication! 1 Corinthians 5-6 tells us to; "Put that person OUT the Church" [no exceptions]. When did the glory of a big wedding cancel out God's Law? This has always been a no, no in the Bible. People were stoned to death for this for over a thousand years in the Bible.

The power of sex has brought down the most famous in Bible. Adam was made perfect yet he disobeyed God for his wife. Sampson the strongest who ever lived and he fell because of sex. David a man after God's own heart fell because of sex. He looked and entertained sin too long, until it was unstoppable. James tells us we sin when we are; "Drawn away of our OWN lusts". David looked to long! Solomon was the wisest who ever lived yet could not and would not deny his sexual needs. The list is long. If the devil sees we are weak in any area that's what he will come at us with. And he always starts with the physical needs. The first temptation he brought to Jesus as His HUNGER. "Turn these stones into bread".

Solomon in Proverbs gives many references about how women tempt men in many ways. "The adulterous woman will seek the precious [a man with morals and convictions] life". "By means of a whorish woman a man is brought to a piece of bread [to nothing]". The devil has billions of women unsaved who he can send at Christians back to back. He will send them our weakest point. Sex can not only ruin your life but kill you. Many have killed and died for sex. It is so powerful Christians need to be ready for it at all times. We need to have on the "whole armor of God" [at all times]. The devil waited 40 days to tempt Jesus because he wanted to do it when he was at his weakest point.

Paul tells us in 1 Cor. 7 about marriage that; "To avoid fornication let every man his OWN wife & every woman her OWN husband". It is perfectly ok to marry for sex. Yes we love whoever we marry as the Bible says. Paul is the one who said; "Let it not once be named among you as becomes Saints". As I said at the start this is a subject that should not even have to be written. If we bend this Law we find ourselves bending many others. What is the problem here? God gives us a way to do this; MARRY! Adultery is sex while married. Fornication is sex when neither is married. Both had the equal punishment; stoned to death. And we also should not have to say that ALL homosexuality is sin! Even church people call and ask where this is written? It's in many places but Romans 1 gives us the clearest wording in the New Testament.

As I said today's modern morals have tried to water down Gods rules on sex out of wedlock. It is never ok. "Jesus the same yesterday, today & forever". In Revelation speaking of those who went to the Lake of Fire it tells of "whoremongers". It puts the blame also on the men that use these women. When we get weak and tempted to fornicate what has also happened is we are losing our FAITH in Christ. Our crime will be against Christ. As David said about his; "Against THEE [God] only have I sinned". We let Jesus down along with the whole Christian Family. The unsaved see this and say; "That's why I don't become one, it doesn't work". They do the SAME as we do. And it's proved all over the news all the time. Preachers and Pastors also preying on the women in the Church. Not just the Catholic Church, but all churches if you watch the news. We do have the power of the Holy Spirit to NEVER fall for this sin.

Today we have denominations that are supper hard on sexual sins yet they have great sins of their own. Jesus told those who were going to stone the woman caught in Adultery; "Let he who is without sin cast the first stone.. And wrote on the ground". I say He was writing other sins in the dirt that the crowd was guilty of worthy of death also. These Churches that extremely condemn gays and other immoral sex are themselves guilty of racism, which is a Proud Look! We cannot point fingers when we are also in the wrong. Racial hatred lead to murders of many people! When we hear Churches call for death of gays they are extremely wrong. Jesus said "Ye know not what Spirit ye are of"? New Testament Christians do not kill for sin. We leave it to the Judgment where no one gets away with nothing. "Whatsoever a man sows that shall he also reap". Which is worse; murder or sexual sin? Both send you to hell. This is what we choose when we vote, because parties are wrong according to the Bible

Anyone that thinks they have an excuse to fornicate will get their feelings hurt at Judgment. Our high tech age does not change God's law. We do not do this because HE said do NOT do it; period! We are looking at HIM and Heaven nothing else. "If you love ME, keep My commandments". We prove if we are serious, or a lukewarm Christian! We prove if God is more powerful than the devil, and the pretty woman or man the devil sent at us! Real Christians do not deny the power of God. "Greater is He in US". "We are more than conquerors".

How can we keep these temptations from getting to strong? Don't stare to long like David. Yes men will look, but turn away quickly from the devil's bait. We always remind ourselves our wives and marriage vows can never be broken. Sex must be only within a marriage. It takes time to commit sexual sins. We can't fall into sex in an instant. We have time to think. TIME Remember there is no person more beautiful than a man's wife or her husband. With Heaven at stake it should be easy to avoid this. No one is cute enough to Miss Heaven for!

CHAPTER 11

"JUDGE NOT"

Matthew 7:1-5

We all hear these words especially from the unsaved. It seems to be very open and shut, but it's not. I haven't heard explained fully as should be. We always have to examine all the scriptures on this before coming to the conclusion. We must go into Romans and 1 Corinthians to get the full understanding. In 1 Cor. 5-6 we are told we ARE to JUDGE! In Romans 14 we see things we are NOT to Judge. There is a distinct difference in the 2 things being done by believers. But first let's see what Jesus meant here when He said Judge not.

The simple fact is the Bible will judge us all anyway. So we as Christians ONLY judge what the Bible says and that makes it NOT OUR JUDGMENT by God's! If we judge or accuse someone of anything not written we have made ourselves a JUDGE. The unsaved use that a lot against Christians when they tell them of any of their wrongs. First off we should not even tell them much about their wrongs because that's what sinners do. They SIN! What we need to tell them is their need for salvation by Jesus Christ, not their wrongs. The story of Jesus shows why He came; to pay for all human wrongs [sins]. We are told to judge those who claim to be Christian. That's 1 Cor. 5-6. "If any man is called a BROTHER; and be a fornicator etc." we put that person out of our company and Church. Pastors don't put out many people anymore because that's cash money their losing.

1 Corinthians 5:12-13; "Them that are without [unsaved] God judges". So we not to be hard on the unsaved but the saved. Romans 8 tells us "They cannot please God" anyway. Christians love to point the finger at sinners while accepting wrongs from those IN the Churches. When I say sinners I'm not putting myself in a higher place, I say that because the Bible never calls us sinners after we are saved. We are called from then on SAINTS! We cannot win souls by shoving their sins down their throat. We are to be gentle with our words as Jesus was. "Let your speech be always with grace seasoned with salt". It was the Leaders Jesus was hard on as we should be. But 99.9% are too afraid to challenge a Pastor. I know that because Rev. 2 the first Church is the only ones who ARE doing it. And they are the 144,000. "Thou has tried them who say they are apostles [True leaders of the Church] and found them LIARS". Our greatest enemy will not be the unsaved but the same ones who gave Jesus the most trouble; Church people! It is the False Prophet in Rev. that causes more damage than the 666 beast.

Looking closer at Matt. 7 we see; "Whatever measure we mete it shall be measured to us again". When we go off the Bible and judge someone by what we in particular don't like, we have made ourselves a judge. If we judge other by what some Denomination said is sin and it is NOT, we take on the false judgment and sin of that Denomination. "If the blind lead the blind BOTH fall". If we were blind that what they said was wrong and we repeat it we are also wrong! Speaking in tongues is one wrong, many think is right. Each denomination has something specific to them. Be careful not to push anything you aren't sure of or you are guilty also. If we start telling condemning people about thing's Jesus didn't say He will Judge US harshly in the same way; "It shall be measured to YOU again". There are things that are not healthy, but are not sin either. Smoking and drinking is a favorite Christians like to condemn. The Bible speaks against being drunk, not drinking. Smoking causes cancer, but so do many other things. Up to the recent 60's every new thing was a sin to the church. TV, movies, dancing, etc. Here a sin there a sin everywhere a sin sin!

We go to Romans 14 the whole chapter to see what we do NOT judge. Paul lists several things from drinking wine to Sabbath days. But in verse 14 he says; "I KNOW and am persuaded by Jesus Christ that there is NOTHING unclean of ITSELF; but to the person who THINKS it's unclean, to HIM it is unclean". This proves something can be a sin for ME but not for YOU. The Lord doesn't want me to drink at all anymore. But I can't tell everyone else not to drink because I can't. There is a lot of FREEDOM in Christ from the strict Law. We can enjoy many things we couldn't before. Verse 22; "Happy is he who condemns not the things he allows". Once we KNOW the scriptures we see many things are not sin to us. Remember in verse 1; "They that WEAK in the faith [understanding of the scriptures]. These are Christians that don't understand and are so fearful they don't eat meat and many other things. Paul had to deal with these UN learned Christians as WE must be gentle with them also.

Many will not accept even seeing these scriptures. So let's look at Mark 7:18. Jesus was speaking of eating with unwashed hands. He told the Pharisees; "There NOTHING from without a man can defile him". Even the 12 didn't quite understand. So He made it super plain. "Whatsoever THING from without, which enters him can NOT defile him". Wow! That covers about everything. Some will get crazy with that, but we know Jesus is saying a SIN is committed, not eaten. It comes from their heart [mind] where the real evil is. "Unto the pure all things are PURE". So back to judging, we stay with the Bible says and never use our own likes and dislikes. We make ourselves as bib a False Preacher when we take their false words and spread them as REAL. We can and will MISS Heaven for doing this. If we aren't sure don't say it.

The last part of Matt. 7:1-5 tells us; "First take the beam out of our own eye so we can see clearly". Once we see that ONLY what the Bible says we can say, we will always be a WRONG Judge! When we just use the Bible we are never wrong OR a Judge. Because we didn't JUDGE it, GOD did! Even when we see a brother sin we are to be gentle Galatians says. We consider if it was US who fell astray. God has set a day to Judge, and until then He is being nice to us all hoping we will get right. But at Judgment all niceness is GONE. We will be judged by what we DID, and none of it is nice. "Weeping and gnashing of teeth". We will MISS Heaven!

Matthew 18:35; "Forgiveness"

"If we forgive not from our HEARTS, every trespass of our brother; neither will our Heavenly Father forgive US". Some things are too hurtful for us to be around a person. But we do forgive them from the bottom of our heart. Jesus said divorce can be ONLY for fornication. Because He made us and KNOWS THAT is too much for even some Christians to bear. Rapes, murders etc. are things we don't have to be around the person ever again. They should be put OUT your Church anyway. They be forgiven and go to another Church. We will MISS Heaven if we fail to REALLY forgive, and God knows our hearts.

CHAPTER 12

"THINKS NO EVIL"

1 Corinthians 13:5

In 1 Cor. There are several things mentioned as proofs of LOVE that all Christians should show all the time. 2 Timothy 3:1-5 Paul tells of horrible personality traits in Christians in these last days. Corinthians tells us how we should be! We will focus on one thing said in verse 5; "Thinketh no evil". Can anyone control what comes in their minds? Thoughts are non-stoppable. All we can do is NOT act on the bad ones. We can get so mad at an incident that it's hard not to act in a sinful way. Romans 12:18; "If it be possible; with all that lies in you; live peaceably with all men". Sometimes it may not be possible. James tells us; "Who can control the tongue?" And how a powerful and deadly member it is. If the tongue is uncontrollable except by the Holy Spirit, how much more NON control do we have over invisible thoughts? So how does a Christian "think no evil"? Or how does this work?

The Bible interpreter gives and explanation as; "remembers no evil" [wrongs someone has done to you]. You can use that also, but I personally see it deeper. I see it as PLANS no evil! Or PLANS to do no evil in retaliation to someone. The Bible tells us; "Offences WILL come". "Be angry and sin NOT". So yes we will be constantly hit with evil harassments from both saved and unsaved. Constantly! Jesus said we will be; "Hated of ALL men". So we should expect to be on guard not to retaliate. This goes even back to the Sermon on the Mount where Jesus warns us about; "Looking at a woman to lust after her". That is thinking evil! Or hating, or seeking and wishing bad to come to those who wronged us. It's all thinking evil. How do we avoid this trap set by Satan from his humans at us?

There are some Christians who came from a violent back ground where they [we] DID use violence all the time when we were wronged. So it surely crosses our minds almost every time it happens. Many Christians come from or still are IN prisons. Violence is a way of life BEFORE we come to Christ. It took God almost a year to take that vengeance out of me. He could have done it instantly like He did my other super bad habits like drugs and liquor. But He wanted to see if "I" was serious about Him and His power. We have to pray for these things to be taken from us. I couldn't even sleep well for a week thinking of the wrong a guy just SAID to me after salvation. All I could think of what I would have done, and still wanted to do. The devil knew how I used to be and tried his best to get me to sin. But I truly loved God and fought it with everything in me. Then about a year later a woman I had helped a lot stole my watch. But this time immediately I had sympathy for HER, not myself. I knew what God would do to her one day for that and I felt sorry for HER! I knew then that the Lord had removed my extreme mind set vengeance. My; "Thinking Evil" was severely reduced. Yes things do come up, but I can handle it now. I used to think I heard God saying; "You aren't going to do anything Freddie, so just stop it". He was right, my love for Him was greater than need for revenge. I would have MISSED Heaven, even though I was a faithful church goer.

We should always consider other Christians past before we set a standard. MOST do not come from violence, and just talk about vengeance. But some really have DONE the physical harm numerous times. There's a prison and street rule; "Don't let nobody get away with nothing never". It truly makes that kind of person sick to his stomach to let a person get away. I was on a freeway after I couldn't catch a guy, but the anger was so bad I got off, went back and caught him. It was not nice what I did! We have all kinds in the church Jesus changed. Paul was one, and the man so crazy he broke chains and went naked. Paul never could fully stop the pain of things he did to Christians before he was saved. Those thoughts WILL come and it's like Paul said; "The messenger of satan" [sending them]. Homosexuals, etc. can never completely beat those thoughts. So we by the Holy Spirit learn to deal with it. Our love for Christ is more powerful than our will to go back in sin. No human is worth going to hell for. When we are saved God brings our guilt level down to where we can deal with it. It is power to help us stay with the Lord. "When we are weak, HE is strong" [in us].

1 Thess. 5:21; "Abstain from all appearance of evil". This goes with the thinking of evil also but the visible part. 1 Cor. 9 Paul says; "When he was with Jews he did as the Jews; and with others he did as the others". Does that make Paul a hypocrite? No! Paul knew many things were not sin, so as not to hurt the weak brothers faith he didn't do what they didn't do [while he was there with THEM]. So if we see a Christian drinking or smoking do we say; "He shouldn't do it because it APPEARS evil"? Where do we draw the line? They called Jesus a "winebibber, friend of sinners". Did he stop dealing with sinners or drinking wine? No! We do like Paul did. When around them don not do certain things that offend them. Paul said; "If meat offend his brother he would never eat meat". Did he stop eating meat? Or did he stop eating it around THEM? Romans 14:22; "Happy is he who condemns not the thing he allows". Romans 14:14; "To him that thinks something is unclean, to HIM it is unclean".

Our thoughts of evil are different. Real Christians don't purposely do evil. But there are some who see what a person does may call it evil. Can we play card games; or go to a movie etc.? If we have a pure heart we can do about anything within reason. "Unto the pure all things are PURE". Christians who truly follow Christ's should always check the Sermon on the Mount several times a year. It tells us what Jesus added to the Law for HIS New Covenant. We don't just NOT do sin, we don't entertain the thoughts of the evil! When evil thoughts pass into our minds we **usher those right along their way back OUT!** We never look to long at women or any temptation to the point it takes control. "We are tempted when we are DRAWN away of our own lusts". We won't get drawn away if we send the evil thought back OUT. When things unique to our background come up we can focus on that main fact; we want GOD more than the evil! No one can stop a thought. But we have power to defeat the wrong ones! Romans 6:14 "Sin shall NOT have dominance over you [anymore]". God "remembers our sins NO more". So the guilt is gone also. The devil cannot get a foothold into us if we let; "HE that is greater in us" [do His job]. Every evil thought the devil brings is a LIE anyway. It won't work. Every lie the devil tells is wrapped up in **a little** truth. The lie he told Eve was partly true. She wasn't going to die RIGHT THEN [surely die]. But she died!

Our enemy works 24-7 thinking of ways to trick us. We need to stay in the Word to defeat all his fiery darts. Or we will MISS Heaven!

CHAPTER 13

"EXAMINE YOURSELVES"

2 Corinthians 13:5

Paul is speaking to the Church here telling them to examine themselves. Why? They were all baptized and accepted Christ? But they were speaking badly about Paul, so he knew something must be wrong with their walk with the Lord. There are many ways to notice something is not right with a Christian. In Acts 19:1-7 Paul met some followers of Apollos and noticed something. So he asked them if they had received the Holy Spirit since they believed. They said they had not even heard of any Holy Ghost. So he baptized them in Jesus name and they received Him. But what did Paul see? We must be absolutely right in our doctrine to see clearly any tares in the Churches. Jesus said don't try to separate them because He knew MOST would get it wrong. Now Jesus also said; "First remove the beam from your own eye that you may see clearly to remove from another's eye". Some things are obvious some aren't.

We will look closer at this because we all should continuously examine ourselves. There is too much at stake and we get no second chance at Heaven. We hear those who never go to Church say; "I'm a Church unto myself; and God knows my heart etc." So we know they are not in the Faith. But what about those confessed baptized believers? Somehow they seem to think they can never go wrong because most Preachers tell them it is done! And they are sealed, and no one's perfect. The truth is MOST will go off course, and most right away. How you ask? When we are first saved we are pure and undefiled because we were saved by the Word. It's after we accept that we start immediately following NOT Christ, but whatever denominational Church we were going to. Jesus said; "Learn of [from] ME" and "My sheep hear My voice". We have the in dwelling Holy Spirit to teach and guide us. It is great if we were back then when the Apostles were mostly in charge and very little false teaching was out there. But now there are way more false, than true teachers. Jesus said; "Many false Prophets will come and deceive MANY [most]".

Yes it is hard when you are a beginner and everyone is coming at you with what you should do. Many were raised in a certain religion for generations and don't want to go against it. But most just don't have time to read the Bible for ourselves and check what we were taught all those years. We are too busy with life's things. If we had any idea that we could be CAST back by Jesus at Judgment we would take the time and check. But no Church teaches the casting back of saints. All those Jesus said cast, depart, and I never knew you were believers and servants. Rev. 3:16; "I will spit you OUT My mouth". If you are IN Christ you are saved; yet they were spit out. If we just remember that we can more understand scriptures.

Let's look at the story of the blind man in John 9. The healing of him was only a small part of the story. The main part was the harsh harassment he and his parents received from the religious Leaders! They hit them hard for saying Jesus had done the miracle. They said; "None of the Leaders have believed Him so they shouldn't either". They jumped on his parents also. They even put them OUT the Church. Remember Jesus said about real Christians; "They will put you OUT the Churches". I been run out of about 8. What about you? Jesus knew who would give believers in HIM the most trouble; Church people! And it is very hard for a beginner. You have to go against the majority. Luke 14:28; "Which of you intending to build a tower sits not down first and counts the cost". It goes on to explain an army of 20,000 coming against you with only 10,000. It's showing we will be outnumbered all the time. We are on the narrow road, and there are way more on the broad road. We are the FEW, they the MANY.

This is the reason so, so many will be lost Jesus said. Fear of being in the minority. Where is the boldness of the Holy Spirit? He is ready and willing to go against them all. I was raised in a certain denomination also. Both my mother and fathers side were tongue speakers. It's all I knew growing up. When I got grown and came back to the Lord I RE checked everything they said and found many things were not biblical. They came at me hard also. They told me [in so many words] what God did was good, BUT now let us tell you how to get it even better. I may have said before I was a Junkie, alcoholic, criminal, and mental patient for 31 years! They could not do anything to help me. Now that God worked a miracle here they come wanting to FINE tune me. I said No thanks; I'll stick with the Spirit that did the miracle! It has been 18 years of doing God's work at full speed. They still don't understand how I have the power to stay saved without tongues. I could teach the whole study about all those gifts, but I won't in this book. I'll only say God can do all those things still, and does. But He does NOT give those gifts to men anymore. He will work through any human at His own discretion. When people see mostly fake miracles being done they flock to those Churches. "And deceive MANY".

Just think if so, so many are fooled by these amateur false Preachers, what will happen when the REAL False Prophet of Revelation 13:11 comes in? They will fall like dominoes! Matthew 24:24; "Many false prophets will come showing GREAT signs and wonders that IF it were possible would deceive the very elect". It is impossible to trick a real Christian! "A stranger they will NOT follow". That Holy Spirit in us all tries to warn us of false teachings, but most will not heed that Voice because of the peer pressure. That is pure FEAR. And Rev. 21:8 speaking of those who went to the Lake of Fire, before it mentions any 10 commandment sin it mentions the "Fearful". There are no cowards in Christ! We die saying the truths. Many were "Beheaded for the Word of God and testimony which they HELD [fast to]". These proved their loyalty to Christ so well HE put them up to do the judging. Rev. 20:4;

"Judgment was given unto THEM". They wouldn't dare let a relative or anyone in Heaven if they didn't follow Christ. They proved while on earth whose side they were on. They went against family and friends and Leaders. So next time someone says; "Only God can judge me", show them Rev. 20:4. He also said; "the men of Nineveh will stand up in judgment with this generation and condemn it". Who is doing the condemning? The men of Nineveh.

Let's look even deeper at examining ourselves. Do we realize the Muslins and Buddhist and Hindu's have been in their religions 1,000's of years. How can we tell them to RE check when we won't even re-check what we been in a few hundred years. Why tell the JHW to check again and we won't? I re-check myself several times to make sure my thoughts are still in line like the Sermon on the Mount teaches. When we have a test in school and get done early, we have time to take a second look and check our answers. We get no second chance at Heaven. There is the new Earth for those too lazy or too scared to re-check. But look what you must go through to get that. Jesus sent them to. "Outer darkness where there was weeping and gnashing of teeth". Gnashing of teeth is because of the pains. But the weeping is because of the hurt devastated feelings. Can you imagine having looked forward to something for 40+ years and get to the end and be told; "I never knew you". That's why Jesus said; "GREAT was the [hurt feelings] fall of that house".

Ezekiel 3:18-21 God tells him; "If he does not warn the unrighteous their blood will be on his hands". Then he goes on to say; "If he fails to warn the Righteous when they fall away, their blood also will be on HIS hands". It is not just the people tails on the line it's the Pastors! And Pastors will judged much stricter. 1 Cor. 3:17; "If any man defile the temple [Christians under their teaching with false doctrine] him will God destroy" they go to the Lake of Fire. Not even the New Earth for them. It they caused 1,000's to miss Heaven they deserve the Lake. Oh if Preachers only KNEW what they are messing with? I am scared to death to teach wrong, and all should be. I know what's at stake for me. Ezekiel was told to warn the righteous also. Most think once they are saved no one can tell them anything because they are IN. Paul and Peter and John kept writing back to the Churches they had been to correcting things they were getting wrong. Remember Paul said; "Oh foolish Galatians; who has bewitched you". They had gotten off track bad. So did the Corinthian Church as this chapter says; "Examine yourselves".

I often say; "I'd rather get my feelings hurt now before judgment and correct it. Than get to judgment where it's too late! Don't we know Jesus prays while we are In Church we will read one day and light will go off and we will correct our beliefs? We cannot take the word these denominations. There is only ONE Church and it's a Spiritual body. Jesus knows who is right in Him and will not spit those out at judgment. But He hopes more will see the light. You are already in the right place. Just stop believing everything said from the pulpit. A real Christian can go to any Church. He goes because we are commanded to assemble ourselves together. But we know the difference in true and false preaching. If we find one of the very few true Pastors with no other ulterior motives like money or following a denomination GOOD. But they are very few. We don't go and disrupt a service, we wait till after and confront the teacher politely about the scriptures. They'll most likely kick you out anyway, but we are told to speak up for truth. John 7:7 & 17; "The world cannot hate you but Me it hates; because I testify [speak up] of it that their deeds are evil". "If any man will "DO" the will of the Father "HE" shall KNOW of the doctrine". God does not show the mysteries to Christians who won't get out there and speak them boldly!

We have today the so called conservative and liberal Churches. They are both wrong in many ways. But let's ask a question of both. If a homosexual accepts Christ and is baptized and goes home to sleep again with their same sex partner, did the salvation really take? Again a Racist get baptized and accepts Christ and goes home still hating people of color did his salvation take? Each side accepts one of these horrible things in Christians as ok. So how can we join either one of them?

Many should re-check and be re-baptized! Don't take any chances with eternal life. Many were baptized to young and didn't fully understand what they were doing and didn't OBEY the Bible. They never stopped sinning. You have time now to do it over, and right this time. Pastors who have preached and now see they were preaching wrong can correct it. Forget your ego and get right while there's time. Or you will MISS Heaven.

CHAPTER 14

"STARS FALL FROM HEAVEN"

Matthew 24:29

This is a mystery the Lord wanted us eventually understand. And now is the time. We know stars are way too big and too HOT to fit on this small earth. So Jesus is speaking of stars as a symbol for something else. Christians have read over this for thousands of years but never took the time to pray for the answer. I wrote in my last book that it's no harm in not knowing the mysteries of Last Days because it was NOT meant to be reveal until NOW. If people in the past had known about the Beasts and Image etc. they would have been focused on what was going to happen instead of what is happening to them and winning souls in their time. Plus "I" say God wanted to expose the FALSE Preachers. These false Pastors and scholars have written many books on the last days because it is popular and sells millions. But they are all GUESSES! So when the truth comes out they all will be exposed as fakes, and God was NOT talking to them. I said before when we study any Bible subject we must take all the scriptures on that subject and see if they ALL fit to our answer. If one doesn't fit it is wrong!

The Stars Falling from Heaven is mentioned more than just Matt. 24. It's in Revelation and Daniel. The scholars never took a guess at this but interpreted the; "Dragons tail drawing a third of the stars and cast them to earth" [Rev. 12:4]. Let's just check that one for now.

They say it's one third of the angels siding with satan. Now this is in the very last time of earth, so why would a third of God's angels rebel when they KNOW the punishment of those angels who sided with satan earlier? It doesn't make even human sense. When scholars come up with an answer they usually check with OTHER scholars to see if they can get some back up. If enough agree they will write and say it as truth. They have man's ok, not Gods. I wrote to a large ministry years ago about Christians being CAST back and he wrote me saying; "NO respectable scholar holds this view". So we see they depend on each other. I also know they all hope Jesus returns before the truth comes out about Revelation so they will NOT be exposed. But this is what Gods plan was all the time. The let them stick their own foot in their mouth. They can be forgiven and get right, but MOST will NOT. Their ego and reputation is on the line. They'd rather take their whole Church than to admit they were wrong.

Jesus said; "Stars Fall from Heaven". So what are these symbolic stars? Revelation 6:13 also speaks of stars falling "as untimely figs" to earth. It cannot be real stars we know. It cannot be angels because they already see the fate of those who rebelled. So for another perspective on this we go to the prophetic book of Daniel 8:10. "It cast down SOME of the HOSTS and of the STARS to the ground and STAMPED on them". We have the best clue ever right here. We see it was SOME not all the stars. And it calls them HOSTS also. Our last clue is STAMPED on them. Where do we remember someone being stamped on? Rev. 11:2; John is told NOT to count those outside the Temple and Altar and; "The Holy city they TREAD under foot 42 months". Are we using our Spiritual eyes now? Can we see this is not angels?

These ARE the cast BACK mislead, sinned willfully, unworthy, no fruit, lazy Christians being rejected ate the "Judgment Seat of Christ". That's why Jesus says CAST them. But where are they being cast FROM, and where TO? That was one of the first things that caught my attention years ago and I prayed until it was revealed to me. The Judgment does not happen while we are on earth or there would be no need to CAST them here. The 7 plagues of wrath haven't been poured out yet, so earth still has life on it. Jesus said the angels would separate them, but where? Now we go to Rev. 14:14-19 and see Jesus about to Rapture the whole Church. Good and bad; [2 Cor. 5:10]. Yes even the BAD Christian's must go UP. There we see "another angel come with a sharp SCIKLE also". But he is told to CAST, not REAP like Jesus did. He casts FROM up there in the clouds, unworthy Christian's BACK to earth where the GREAT Trib. Is about to start, and ALL down here will die! It is called outer darkness, fire, and HELL [for the still living]. Jesus gave 2 examples of hell. One the rich man "died" and was buried, so we know that's a hell for the dead. Then in Mark 9 He gives another example but his time the peoples "worms dies NOT". So they are not dead! What makes those still living the same as the DEAD in hell? Those who are alive when the Rapture comes can SEE then that God is REAL. We are saved by FAITH. So once they see it, there is no more faith involved and no can be saved period. They are just like the dead in their hell; they cannot be saved either. Rev. 7:14 speaks of Tribulation Saints, but these ARE those cast BACK who were saved before the Rapture when Faith was still possible. No one unsaved can get saved at that time!

Why did it takes all these years to see this? God doesn't need an earthly trained scholar. He is the teacher [1 John 2:27]. He needs a willing heart. You can't put "New Wine in old bottles". If they are full of human knowledge God can't get HIS in there. Paul was so full of earthly schooling God had to send him away 3 years to get that JUNK out of him before He could use even use him! It's the same today. People want to go to human schools to get the prestige and praise of MEN, not God. I only got to the ninth grade in school, yet God uses me. Or you can use it as an excuse to disregard me. "Not many wise after the flesh are called".

Let's go to the scripture that should clench this about who the stars are. Daniel 12:3; "They that be wise shall SHINE as the brightness of the firmament; and they that turn MANY to righteousness as the "STARS" forever". Isn't this a clincher? God is referring to HUMANS as STARS! And it said SHINE bright [like stars]. I was not going to go deep into my last book about Revelation and the mysteries explained. But I had to put this in because it shows Christians MISSING Heaven in detail. It was meant to come out NOW and you see it. Please do not take your salvation lightly thinking you are a shoe in for Heaven. Every time Jesus mentions Heaven He ADDS something like; "Sells all; forsakes all etc." Not the saved but "Lukewarm" [average]. To be HIS disciple we hear His voice, not the denominations. And strangers we "will NOT follow".

John 3:16 says if we just believe, we get eternal life and that's true. But where we get that eternal life is up to US. If we are lazy with HIS work and sin willfully we cannot expect to get the same reward as those who forsook ALL. God is a righteous Judge and knows how to issue rewards and punishments justly. We all can make Heaven that's why Jesus ONLY spoke of Heaven. He did not speak of 2nd place; the New Earth, because we ALL can make Heaven and "His yoke is EASY" not hard.

Now that you see more details of how the Judgment will work there's no reason or excuse for anyone reading this book to Miss Heaven.

CHAPTER 15

"WORSHIP IN VAIN"

Matthew 15:8-9

Jesus is warning people in "advance" that most would be worshiping Him for nothing! If you try and say He was talking to the Leaders only, keep reading. He says farther down; "If the blind lead the blind BOTH fall into the ditch" [of hell]. We know the unsaved don't worship Him at all, nor even go to Church. So He must be speaking of believers. I have repeated in this book over and over about people getting their feelings hurt at Judgment. Why is it so hard to accept the facts? Most Christians know this seems true but still will not change. There is a scripture in Isaiah 30:10 that's interesting about this; "Prophesy NOT unto us RIGHT things, speak unto us SMOOTH things, prophesy LIES". They just don't want to hear the truth, it's too hard and will alter their lives. When we want something to be a certain way bad enough we will believe it even if it is coming from known LIARS!

So we can't fully just blame the Leaders. It's the people that are asking for the easy parts only. 2 Timothy 4:3; "They will heap to themselves teachers having itchy ears". Meaning the Leaders will listen to what the people WANT, and preach accordingly. If one Church preaches the hard truths, they are many others who they can go to and not hear about their sins. Churches have become money making organizations. All the Apostles warned of this. Pastors work for money not Christ. They are called "hirelings" by Jesus in John 10. Jeremiah 23 is a whole chapter on God saying how even back then "I have not sent them"; "They preach a vision of their OWN heart". If you can't name 20 false preachers on TV, how do you know you're not following one? We should be able to name 100 on TV!

These are the same people in Matt. 7 who Jesus told; "Depart from Me, I never knew you". Feelings hurt! Everyone Jesus cast out and back seemed so surprised; why? Just like us they had their instructions in advance. It was them who chose not to obey them. Just like us today we think God will give us a BREAK at Judgment. It's not fair to the ones who did obey and sacrificed. I tell my friends who outright sin and still say they going to heaven; "If you get in, look around because Hitler and Nero will be coming also". If any sinner got in they all can get in. But oh 2 Peter says; "We look for New Heavens and New Earth, wherein dwells righteousness". And Rev. 21:27; "Nothing that is defiled shall enter its gates, but he whose names are in the LAMBS book of life". Rev. 3:4-5 Jesus speaks of BLOTTING names out of His book! Yes just like your name goes IN, it can be taken OUT! Just like we are "Changed in a moment in the twinkling of an eye"; we can be changed BACK in the twinkling of an eye and sent back down. Hurt feelings galore. What really makes it hurt is we did hear the truth and didn't recognize it. We were not Jesus sheep because "His sheep hear his voice".

Most Christians I assume don't gamble. This is worse than going to Vegas and betting your house that you worked years to pay off on one roll of the dice. We wouldn't do that, yet we bet our eternal life. If someone says they are going to KILL you, you take steps to prevent getting killed. You call the police; buy a gun; don't go certain places etc. But God says He will kill you we don't take it serious. What more can He do? Isaiah chapter 5 God tells the story of a Vineyard He built. He says He watered, fenced and did everything for it. Then when it was time to harvest the grapes He said; "It brought forth WILD grapes". Grapes like any other vineyard that didn't have all that done for it. He asks; "What more could He have done for that vineyard that He didn't do?" He said; "You be the Judge"? The Jews had no answer. Now in the New Testament we have the same thing. Jesus came and showed His power by the Father. He gave men the gifts of miracles also. He left 12 then 120 to start the Church, and the Holy Spirit. And look what kind of Christians it has produced? Christians today will cuss and lie and hate and fornicate JUST like the unsaved world. What more could He do for the Church. He gave His LIFE even.

"How can we escape if we neglect so great a salvation" Hebrews. 2:3? All these scriptures I shouldn't even have to write for Christians. You should know them all. But most Christians get BORED by to many scriptures. That's why many Preachers don't preach a lot of scriptures. They get up and quote 2-3 scriptures then tell a story about their fishing trip, or something that will keep your attention. It's the WORD that saves and keeps us, and gives us MORE Faith to endure to the end. The more scriptures we get IN us the more Faith we will have. [If we are OBEYING them]. Many quote them but don't do them. The last part of Matt. 7 Jesus tells a story of 2 houses. One built on sand the other on a rock. The one on sand fell and GREAT was the fall. He said the rain and wind and flood BEAT on BOTH houses. He said BEAT! Warning us we don't know how much faith we will need so get EXTRA. The parable of the 10 Virgins in Matt. 25 where 5 didn't bring any EXTRA oil and their lambs went out. They got to the wedding to late and the door was SHUT. He would not left them in. Can't we see how all this is for us and not just a story for them? We should always put ourselves in all the Bible stories. Those words transcend time and are for our modern age just like it was for them. Men's hearts and minds have not changed.

That first part of Matt. 15 tells how Jesus got to telling the story of worshipping in Vain. He called it the "Tradition of the Elders". Or as I have been saying following any denomination. That is tradition. Let's just say one of the 150 or so denominations is true because there is only one church. So it means every one of the other 149 is going to Miss Heaven and go to hell. So which one would it be? The problem is almost none will go that far to say all the rest will go to hell. They all now see flaws in what they have been preaching and now want to get together and say; "We all worship the same God, and He will excuse us because we tried, and no one's prefect". Wow! Is that the best we can come up with? Will we risk our eternal future on that? What we are telling God is it's HIS fault we can't figure out the truth. We are going to blame Him like Adam did. "That woman YOU gave me; she gave me the fruit". Excuses will not work. Yes it's hard to go against something we been in all our lives, but we must do it. Isn't a city of GOLD worth the extra study? Are you doing what the people in Matt. 22 did; "Made light of it". That's why most will miss Heaven. They just do NOT have time to check. It's the preacher's job they say.

Many will say at Judgment; "That's what the Pastor told me". It won't work. "If the blind lead the blind BOTH fall". As I said earlier Church Leaders go to the Lake of Fire. No New Earth for them like there will be for you after hell. That's 1 Cor. 3:14-17. The man in 14 gets a reward [Heaven]. The man in 15 gets NO reward, but is saved [AFTER] he goes through [another] FIRE. Verse 13 we ALL go through the first fire of the regular Tribulation. But the guy in 15 must go through another FIRE; the GREAT Tribulation where everyone dies! But the guy in verse 17 God "Destroys". He gets no reward nor is he even saved! And even those cast back will AGREE with his punishment because he is the one who got sent to hell on earth. He is the one who made them MISS Heaven. He is the one who took their MONEY while lying and guessing all those years. He is the one who said; "Don't question me"; I have a degree! And it's not as if it was just you, but it will be 1 billion 800 million of you! Of course he deserves the Lake.

Now if you want to look even closer at this you can read Ezekiel chapters 40-48. It tells of the New Earth and what it will be like, even the size of the earthly Temple. But there's something interesting in 44:11-15 speaking of some former Leaders who do get to go there. They must do the Temple work and "Bear their SHAME" for leading the people WRONG! Can you imagine the shame? Because every year they all must go up to the mountain of God where the Holy Jerusalem City of Gold is and stand "outside" and worship. Yes they will be reminded every year of what they MISSED! Those who did take the abuse and were in the minority will be IN that city of GOLD 1,500 miles square. Others can never go IN ever. Read all the chapters 40-48 and see the water that comes under a door in the earthly Temple and turns into a great deep river and dumps into the Dead Sea. Life springs forth everywhere it goes. All water has a source. The water here spiritually comes from the river that flows in the Holy City. The water of LIFE. Beside the river In the City are 2 tress of life on each side of the river.

Now just to think of which city you would want to be in? Jesus ONLY spoke of Heaven because He wanted us ALL to make 1st place and we CAN. He said it's easy not hard. It's only hard if we try to have it both ways. If want to find an easier way to Heaven than His way. I've seen many, and I mean many come to Christianity and think they figured a way to get in without obeying all He said. 2,000 years and THEY figured out an easy way? This is like Acts 5 Ananias and Sapphira his wife. They saw the others selling their land and giving ALL the money to the Church. But they said; "We can LOOK just as righteous as them". So they sold land and gave only a PART of their money. They were smarter than the other Christians and GOD Himself they thought. God struck the both down the same day. Look how many today PRETEND to be just like real Christians. If God was still striking down people the same day there would be no hypocrite's in the Churches. But He has a day picked.

Let's all re-check while there's still time. Even I re-check. The penalty is too high and the reward is too GREAT to take chances. We wouldn't gamble our house, don't gamble our eternal lives and chance MISSING Heaven.

CHAPTER 16

"I NEVER KNEW YOU"

Matthew 7:23

This is a very harsh thing to say to those people who just told Jesus all the things they did in His name. "Prophesied; cast out devils; did many wonderful works". They were Christians when they did these things. They were baptized believers. Yet we remember Jesus said; "In vain they worship ME". Still how can He say He NEVER knew them? We will go straight to the Old Testament for a better explanation. Ezekiel 2:20; "And his righteousness which he has done shall NOT be remembered". That seems wrong to us. But we are not in charge, He is. So let's look at it from HIS perspective.

All through the Bible he tells us the kind of worship and deeds He wants. Even in the Old Testament He told them how He wanted things down to the last detail. He said who was to do the sacrifices and when. He said NO one else, and killed some who were not supposed to do it. He told them the exact measurements of each piece in the Temple and where they were to be placed. He was exact on everything so they couldn't make a mistake. He told Moses and Joshua: "Turn not to the left or the right" [of what I say]. Don't even use your own way of thinking on My rules. "My thoughts are not your thoughts, nor My ways your ways; as high as the Heavens are from the earth so are My ways higher than your ways". Wow; can it be plainer? In the military they take orders period. Officers are not 2nd guessed, and they are mere humans like us.

A GOD is much higher than any King or countries Leader. So why do we second guess God? When don't see Him as the creator of all things then we question Him. But when we realize like He said; "His eyes are in every place", and we believe that we do NOT question Him. He made us and knows us better than we know ourselves. He sees the future and what will happen and we can NOT. So how did Christians who say they believe all this decide they can do His work better than He said do it?

That's what happened to those in Matt. 7:22 doing what THEY called wonderful works. Wonderful according to WHO? They were not in charge! When we don't go by the rules we are eliminated from the race period. All our effort is discarded and not recorded. Ezekiel told them YES they did do some right, but when they started doing wrong it was canceled out. We are told IF we endure to end [doing it right] we shall be saved.

Paul set up many Churches and kept in touch with them to make sure they did not stray away from what he taught them. And we see many did, so he had to write 2nd letters to most of them. He told the Galatians; "Oh foolish Galatians, who has bewitched you". They had strayed from what he told them and listened to the Jews. He asked them ONE question. "One thing would I learn of [from] you; did you receive the Spirit by works or by Faith"? What saved us is what we stay with. I was delivered from 24 years of shooting dope in my arms. Why would I trust anything other than the Spirit that did that miracle?

It is not hard to follow Christ and make Heaven if we just do what He said without our own input. We are like goldfish in a bowl. We see all the things out there in space but have no idea how they got there or what they are made of. Like goldfish we can be killed a thousand different ways by our owners and there's nothing we can do to stop it. Our life is like grass the Bible says. Here today gone tomorrow. How can we control anything when we are on a planet spinning around a sun, in open space? With a moon spinning around us? We have powerful telescopes that been looking in space decades and still haven't found a planet we can live on of the billions out there. Is our one little planet and accident?

Fact is anyone who doesn't believe in a GOD is a fool. And Jesus said "call no man a FOOL". But if a person doesn't believe in GOD there's nothing else to call him but a FOOL. But we are talking about Christians here. Jesus instructions are plainly written. He said it's easy not hard. If others can do them we can too. These people decided they would do things their way. They chose the easy, clean, non-controversial jobs that looked good to men, not GOD. I always say compare these in Matt. 7 to the ones in Matt. 25 who DID get in. "Come ye blessed of My Father". They worked with the POOR, sick, in prisoned, poorly clothed etc. They worked with people Churches today don't want to deal with. The poor! They wanted Jesus to hang with them, not the sinners and poor. Jesus told His 12; "When you give a dinner do NOT invite your rich friends, invite the poor". There are many other stories about how we should deal with the down and out. God said "The poor will never cease out of the land". God takes our Spiritual temperature by how we treat the poor. He could make us all rich, but He wants to see when we stop loving, and helping each other like He commanded us.

So let's stop chancing our own ideas and what the denominations tell us to do. We won't be able to blame them at Judgment. Ezekiel does say; "Their blood He will require at his [Leaders] hand". If leaders lead you wrong or don't tell you the real truth, God will get them ALSO; but worse! Paul said; "I am free from the blood of all men because I failed not to give you ALL Gods message". Leaders today have money on their minds, not Gods punishment. They want to please the people and get their praise, not God's. I'm scared to death to teach wrong. I'd rather the whole world hate me than God tell me; "He doesn't even remember or know me".

We see mega Churches today with bands and great choirs making what seems like joyful noises to God. We see BBQ's bingo, trips to places etc. We see what we think are wonderful works because we do not know our Bible either. Jesus said; "You will know them by their fruit". But if you don't know good from bad fruit; and good from bad preaching you are in trouble! False Preachers use enticing words and have a great motivator; MONEY! Jesus said "If it was possible they would fool His elect [best]".

Here's another hard and serious reason to re-check our scriptures and Church. You may not even be remembered with all your 40+ years of service. That's a lot of wasted time down the drain. Let's examine ourselves so don't; MISS Heaven!

CHAPTER 17

"WEEPING & GNASHING OF TEETH"

Matthew 25:30

It may help if people can see this weeping happening in Revelation to get a better understanding of it. We can see for sure if these people MISSED Heaven. There are 2 places in Rev. that speaks of; "God shall wipe all tears from their eyes". It's in Rev. 7:17 & 21:4. Have you ever wanted to know whose tears He is wiping away? Did we just assume it was those saved during the Great Tribulation? I showed earlier that NO one who was not saved can get saved after the Rapture. Because we are saved by GRACE, through FAITH! Once the world sees the Rapture there is no more faith involved. Faith is believing without seeing.

So who are these people God is wiping tears from? The only people Jesus said would be crying. Those cast into outer darkness where there was "weeping and gnashing of teeth". Their feelings had been greatly hurt after being rejected by Christ, and told He never knew them. But let's look closer at what Rev. 7 says. In verse 14 it tells of them being the ones who; "Came out of GREAT Tribulation". Still how do we know they are Christians? Rev. 2:20-23 Jesus speaks of those who seduce His servants, meaning they were saved. He goes on to say He will; "Cast them into Great Trib.". He goes on to say; "He will kill her [followers of false Preachers] children with death". He also says; "They that commit adultery with her". Adultery is when you are married. They were supposed to be married to Christ. They are the ones He sent into Great Trib.

Let's look at Rev. 21:4 and its reference to who they are. In Chapter 21 the New Earth and Heaven are just now coming in. The real Saints have been up there reigning with Christ the symbolic 1,000 years from the 1st resurrection. This is the 2nd resurrection. God is wiping away their tears before they go to the New Earth. It is plain as day. It's a joyful thing to go to Heaven, not sad. They sing the song of Moses when they went up in Rev. 15. No crying for them. We really need to see this because once we miss out with Jesus, we will be accepted by the Father and be sons of God, not the bride of Christ. They will have new but fleshly physical bodies again. We in Heaven will have Spiritual bodies, and can never die ever again. The others can die if they ever brake God's Laws while down here on the New Earth [Zach. 14:16-19].

But it is the wisdom and love of our God to have come up with this. He knows even with Heaven as a prize MOST will be lazy and too scared to do what He says. If He had not put this in place look how FEW would get eternal life. Rev. 7:9 John says he saw so many no man could even count them all. That's how many get it wrong following false Preachers. Remember the broad and narrow roads. And FEW find LIFE.

But as we said before Jesus wants us all to make Heaven. That's why He only Preached Heaven, because we all can make it. We can never blame God for our weaknesses, because He gave us the POWER with the Holy Spirit who is much stronger than evils. We make Him look bad to the world by not being; "More than conquerors". We have all we need to win this, so why would we MISS Heaven?

CHAPTER 18

"FIRE NOT QUENCHED"

Mark 9:46

I must show the full consequence of Missing Heaven. Most know of these verses in Mark 9 about hell and the "Fire shall never be quenched". What does that mean? Most don't know the difference between the Lake of Fire and HELL. Yes this is hell but this hell is on earth. It is the time on earth AFTER the Rapture. That's when God will pour out His 7 Vails of Wrath on those left on the earth. Rev. 16:6 speaking of when all fresh water is gone it says; "They have shed the blood of Saints and Prophets and thou has given them blood to drink; for ARE worthy". All not taken at the Rapture will be counted guilty of the wrongs done to the Saints over all earths time. Jesus said the same thing to the Pharisees in Matt. 23; "Upon you may come all the righteous blood shed upon the earth". We don't have to think it's fair, God does!

The Lake of Fire doesn't come in until after all are dead on earth when the War of Armageddon takes place. Then the 2nd resurrection of all the dead. But we are going to focus on this hell Jesus is speaking of. It covers verses 43-48, and tells not only of the unsaved going, but warning Christians to "Cut off" their limbs if needed to stay out of this place! He is warning them because as I have been saying many Christians will go also. So if anyone [and I heard some say it] thinks the New Earth is good enough; look what you will have to endure first! This is not the hell of the dead in the ground, but people living on earth.

God will cut off food and water and the sun will get super-hot. The Beast, False Prophet and devil will be in charge down here. Heaven will be sealed up and the door shut. No prayers are getting through. Matt. 25:41; "Everlasting fire prepared for devil and his angels". Most think it the time for the devils punishment, but it's time for them to RULE down here without God interfering for; "A time, times and half a time".

During that set time limit the Fire will not be quenched. Meaning there will be NO relief of the pain, hunger, deaths etc. This is the Spiritual FIRE of hell. God will not send any rain or food. The Beast will be in charge of what little food there is. And he sure won't give any to those cast back Christians unless they get his MARK. This time has many names; outer darkness, furnace, hell etc. But it's not the Lake of Fire. This is the torment before the unsaved even start to pay for their sins. Remember back then they beat and humiliated people before they killed them like they did Jesus. They surrounded a city and let them starve before attacking and killing them. The Lake of Fire is the 2nd death, this is just their first death. When they get to the Lake their time starts on paying for ALL their sins. It's like the county jail. You haven't been sentenced yet. You stay in jail till you go to court and see how much time you will get in PRISON. Prison is the Lake of Fire where your time begins. Yes jail is bad but not as bad as prison.

There will be NO relief of the pain and torment if you are rejected by Christ. The rich man and Lazarus; he asked for a drop of water to cool his tongue. None was given. Read the details; many Christians will go there. We don't want this so let's not MISS Heaven!

CHAPTER 19

"BEATEN MANY STRIPES"

Luke 12:47

Jesus tells us here that some Christians will be punished more than others if they miss Heaven and go to the Great Tribulation. Those in verse 47 are the ones who "knew" the Lords will and didn't do it. Verse 48 tells of those who knew not His will and were beaten with FEW stripes. But both were beaten! Why? I have been saying there will be NO excuses accepted at Judgment; NONE. Those followed False Preachers will not be able to say; "That's what they told me". We have the Holy Spirit as a guide and teacher if we follow our Spirit instead of the denominational Preachers. Yes we grow up IN a certain faith and most don't ever question it. So how does Jesus say who knew, and didn't know?

There are many who will never ever get the real truths from these Churches. Most live way away from main stream preaching anyway. Some places and countries only allow their version of Christianity Preached. Some of the more famous denominations are everywhere, and the smaller ones with MORE [not all] TRUTHS are scarce. For example if a church says worship and pray to Mary; or John Smith got another Bible from Jesus, we know better but they don't. If that's all they ever heard why fault them? We are not God. He knows when His Spirit worked with their spirit and warned them it was false. Every Christian who accepts Christ gets that Holy Spirit period. That's how we are known to be raised at the 1st resurrection; [Ro. 8:11] because we have His Spirit in us. The unsaved don't have it. Rev. 20:5; "The rest of the dead lived NOT until". It's because they do not have His Spirit in them. In the sleep of death we still have that Spirit.

Jesus will look at those who DID hear the truth like those reading this book. Even those who only heard the truths once will be held accountable for that one time. Somewhere in Christians lives they heard truths that went against their denominations, but decided to ignore them. Even the JHW as false as they are have some truths against false Churches. Figure out what the right parts are. Re-read chapter 5 about the Bundles and Clusters. I was raised hearing ONLY those who speak in tongues are really saved. That's what the Corinthian Church thought. They were the only Church with that thinking, no others. Paul was very gentle trying to tell them this was false in 1 Cor. Chapters 12-14. I have heard the best from each denomination trying to win me over. I was always in the minority in each Church once I repented and came back to the Lord 19 years ago. I was kicked out of 7-10 because I wouldn't accept it.

Jesus predicted False Preachers coming. Matt. 24:14 after He mentioned fakes 2-3 times He says; "Before the end **comes THIS Gospel** of the kingdom will be preached to all nations". Not the watered down version that these rich Churches can and have sent around the world. They say Jesus can come at any time now, because the Gospel is gone around the world. Wrong! It is not the real Gospel Jesus was speaking of. The 2 Witnesses and 144,000 will preach the version Jesus Preached. It was 400 years between Malachi and Matthew. In that 400 years without God dealing with the Jews, look how far off the truths they had gotten by the time Jesus came? Now it's been 2,000 years since God sent a Prophet. How far off do you think the Churches have gotten now? A lot! Hebrews 10:26-29; 29 tells us; "how more of a WORSE punishment" Christians will get. It says they; "Trodden underfoot the Son of God".

So when and where will this take place? By now you should know it's the Great Trib. After they are cast back at the Judgment seat of Christ and sent back to earth to die with the sinners of the world. Still how can they be beaten worse, and more than other Christians if they are all starving? God has a way to make anything happen. "All things work together for the good of those love God". We know that down here. And He can make it work in the Great Trib. For those who never got to hear as much as you did. He can provide some more thing's than the average Christian is getting. He can have those who heard more, be captured by the Beast earlier and punished severely. He can do it many ways. If He said you will be beaten MORE, you will be beaten MORE period. Psalms 91 tells us; "A 1,000 shall fall at thy side, and 10.000 at thy right hand, but it shall not come nigh thee". Yes God has the power to issue punishment to the right people.

Revelation 21:8 has a mystery I will show, and is in my last book on Revelation. It says of those go there; "Shall have THEIR part". Their own, individual part of punishment in the Lake of Fire according to how many sins they themselves committed. It's all on record how many and how bad they were, and must be paid for. Then they receive the 2nd death. It's only forever and ever for those who do the 3 things in Rev. 14:9-11. Jesus said; "Every idle word will be brought into Judgment". The person who robs will get less torment than the one who robs and KILLS the person. Jesus said of Judas; "Better he wasn't even born". So we know it was bad on him. Even death is a relief in the Great Trib. Because all on earth will die anyway. May as well get it over with. A person being tortured wishes he had committed suicide before he let them tie him up. Jesus said cut off your hand and foot and pluck out your eye rather than go there.

Those reading this book need to know there are many in the world who will never hear of this book. If some did they would have taken steps to correct their walk with Christ. Many in smaller 3rd world countries will wish they had heard it different. Remember the verse; "He that knew", you know now. Sometimes I feel real bad for the people that hear me because I know it will be harder on them. Even my own children!

Notice also in the 48th verse it says; "To whom MEN have committed much, of him they will ask the MORE". These are those who preach for a denomination [hirelings] that weren't sent by Jesus but still Preach and believe in Him. They have taken on a job that deals with Jesus people. All they lead wrong they are responsible for also. Paul speaks of people preaching for the wrong reasons in Philippians. He says "at least the word is being preached. Why? Because if a person just gets IN the Church they are around the Gospel and SHOULD one day see the real truths and change. All in all denominations have a better chance at Heaven than those who don't even go to Churches.

Yes the Gospel has been greatly polluted and watered down and HIJACKED by some horrible murderous people claiming their saved. God saw this and had a plan. The 144,000 and 2 Witnesses are here, and will start soon. If you don't believe me, you have a chance to believe them and not MISS Heaven.

CHAPTER 20

"FORSAKE ALL"

Luke 14:33

Jesus says forsake all more than once. But how far do we take this? We do have a life with bills and some with a family. The Bible commands us to take care of them or we are "worse than an infidel". So where is the line? As we search the scriptures we see what the main work is He wants done. It's: "The harvest is plentiful, but he laborers are FEW", "Pray the Lord of the harvest send laborers into His vineyard". No matter what lazy Christians tell you this is the job Jesus says needs workers. This means someone must take time out their own agendas to do His work. He told the 12; "I will make you fishers of men". And; "As the Father has sent Me. So send I you" [to work]. Why do most look at this as someone else's job? It's because we don't want to take time out of our lives for Him period. In today's computer age we do have many, many things to do. But if we truly want to please God we need to DO something. John 15:8; "Herein is the Father glorified; that ye bear MUCH fruit". Praise and worship IN Church does not take the place of witnessing! And John 15:2; "Every branch that bears fruit He prunes it to bear MORE fruit". So we see it's about the maximum not the minimum like we want to give. Daniel 12:3; "They that turn MANY to righteousness shall shine as the stars forever".

We can say all we want about the time we have and can spare for His work, but He knows what we can and can't do. He has set a line for each of us and we will be judged by HIS line not ours. The proof of this is in Matthew 25:15 when Jesus gave the parable of the Talents. It says; "He gave them according to their several ability". Because He knows exactly what each of our situations and abilities are. He knows what is considered important for a Christian and what is NOT important. Yes we have our own version of what's important also, but do we have it right? Obviously we don't because He said the laborers are FEW. And even PRAY that the father send laborers! Wow; someone isn't doing their part.

The reason most don't have time is they are chasing the same things of the world sinner's chase. Money, fame, material things and riches. Christians should not even have these desires in their hearts. 1 John 2:15-17; "Love not the world nor the things IN the world; for all that in the world is not of the Father, but of the world". These flashy things the devil puts up as trendy and fashionable is for the unsaved to chase. We do not try to keep up with the Joneses. We "Set our minds on things ABOVE, not on things on the earth". There are so, so many scriptures on this. We go to churches and the parking lot is a car show; and the church a fashion show. Everyone trying to look better than rest. The Bible speaks of dressing in modest apparel. Paul says; "With food and raiment let us therewith be content". Food; not lobster and caviar. Clothes, not expensive outfits. Some have nerve to say they just giving God their best. He said "The poor ye have with you always"; so who are you shaming?

Still I think most Christians want an idea of where the line is even it has to come from me. So staying with the Word let's look closer at some thing's. 1 Cor. 7 Paul speaks of not getting married so you devote your life or more time to God. But many of us are married with families. We had a need for a wife and sex. Paul did see that and said; "If we cannot contain, let us marry". So we are not faulted for that. Let's look at our own schedules and see what we can cut out to give God more time? I cannot judge another Christians schedule. God knows in your life what should have been cut out or reduced. Parents today take children all over town nowadays to sports events etc., and we watch a ton of TV. If you are sports fan the games come on continuously and when one season stops another sports season starts. At 4 hours per game what time do you have left? Yes we all need a break and rest from the madness of each day's events. Jesus even took the 12 to the hills for rest. Our minds and bodies need rest. Jesus sometimes didn't even eat because of the Fathers work. He said; "My meat [food] IS the do the will of Him that sent me". No we cannot be as hard working as Jesus, but we can do as much as we can.

I saw Christians didn't even know how to spread the Word, or were full of fear. Yes we live in a high crime time, but we have a job to do. I wrote a study called "Witnessing without walking". It show ways to set a list of just 5-10 names a month to speak to about Salvation each month. They can be their friends and relatives even in other states. They write, call and send letters even. At least they are doing something! At the end of the month cross off those who show no interest and keep the ones who are at least listening. Add a few more names to make up the 5-10 again the next month. You can get 100 tracts and just see if you have nerve to pass out 10-20 on your daily routine of going to the stores gas stations etc. You can do this in well-lit places where it's SAFE and many people around. You don't have to risk your life. We all have relatives unsaved whose phone numbers we have. We may have not spoken to them in years but we have a decent friendship with them. They would love to hear from you. Some are hurting from this corrupt economy anyway and see no way to get any comfort. We know of the Comforter. We know a Person to cast our burdens on. It's when people are sick and broke and hurting that they turn to GOD. Very few come to God when they are doing well.

This is one Command that we will not be able to get around any longer and say "We didn't know". John 15:2; "Every branch in ME that bears not fruit My Father takes away". Many try to say our fruit is love, joy peace etc. But read that carefully; that's the Holy Spirit's fruit He is producing. It's not ours, it's HIS. He is trying to work through us to SHOW these things, and many won't let Him produce those loving qualities in us. We see some mean quick tempered Christians all over. The Holy Spirit is a SPIRIT and we need flesh and blood to witness to flesh and blood. Stop praying for Jesus to save people. When He was down here He did the footwork, now it's our turn to do the footwork. Most are not evangelists, but we are responsible to give the Word to ALL in our circle of acquaintances. It's not enough to just say; "They see me and I'm always going to Church etc." We must speak UP!

God knows there's real fear in us, but there was real fear in most of them back then also. They faced death and ridicule also. 1 John says; "Perfect love casts out fear". We need to overcome that fear NOW. The devil is counting on our fear and busy schedules to keep us from spreading God's Word to get souls saved. We MUST let our families know we have ANOTHER job also that MUST be done for the Lord. Let's cut out all we can from our daily routines to do His work. He knows what is important and NOT! Who do we love more? Have we forsaken all" for real? Will we let anyone or anything make us continue to not do his work and MISS Heaven?

CHAPTER 21

"MORE THAN CONQUERORS"

Romans 8:37

Paul in these verses from 8:33-39 gives a powerful victory speech. If we can get these words in our spirits we can make this journey easy. Jesus said his yoke is "EASY and burdens light". Not hard and heavy! Peter gives us a list things and says if we do them we will "Never FALL". John says; "Greater is He in us than he that is in the world". Do we really believe the Bible? Why do so many Christians have their heads down in defeat and fear? Why aren't they obeying all He said do? We have all the info and tools needed to win this race. God is not even letting the devil slip anything in on us we were not already warned was coming. In Revelation he gives us a terrifying example of the beast to come. It tells of 7 heads and 10 horns etc. God does this not to scare us but that we get overly prepared for his coming. Daniel gives a more terrifying picture of him. "Dreadful, terrible; devours, breaks in pieces, and stamps the residue under his feet". If you must face something that horrible you should get extra protection. And that's why God describes him like that.

One problem is most Churches Preach Christians will NOT even be here when the beast comes. That's a LIE! I don't have time in this book to cover those scriptures, but they are all in my last book. "They Have Revelation Absolutely Wrong". The devil is banking on Christians not believing they are going into the 1st part of the Tribulation. Yes there are 2 parts; and they don't preach that either. We ALL go into the first part. This is a test for us. It's not the really bad part like the 2nd part where everyone dies that's left on earth. If you don't think you will face this you won't get ready. The devil will catch you unarmed and off guard. You will fall like dominoes, and "Great will be the fall of that house". When we see the 1st century Church went through a Tribulation with Nero killing them by the thousands, what makes you think we are better than them? Read Revelation 6:9-11 where those same Saints are rising at the 1st resurrection and say; "How long will you not judge and avenge our blood". They see it is now 2000 years later and the earth and evil is still going on and God has not avenged them. God says; "They should rest for a season, till their FELLOW servants that should be KILLED "AS" they were [in a Tribulation] should be fulfilled". Oh yes we will be tested also. Rev. 12:11; "They loved not their lives unto the death". If we are afraid of death the devil has us beat. Jesus said we must; "Take up our CROSS". Cross means we will die for this!

So how can we prepare? Paul says "Put on the whole amour of God". This Bible tells us exactly how to win the battle. The whole Bible is full of victories against overwhelming odds. David and Goliath; Gideon; Pharaoh and Moses etc. We are not to look at the physical but the Spiritual. The devil has already been defeated and has been sentenced to eternal torment. All he wants to do now is take as many to the Lake of Fire with him as he can. Remember the demons told Jesus; "Are you come to torment us BEFORE the time"? They know their fate is sealed! The devil is bluff and all bark with no bite. Jesus took the power from him and the KEYS of death and hell. Jesus now says who stays in hell and who doesn't. He has the keys now. Jesus said we can defeat him because HE defeated him. We beat him by Jesus power not our human power. We don't have to fight toe to toe with the devil either. The Bible says just; "Resist the devil and he WILL FLEE from us". Why? Because he has his ORDERS from GOD that he must obey. If the devil could he would kill every one of us before we could repent. We don't talk to him except with scripture like Jesus did when tempted 40 days. Only quote scriptures. That's what he can't fight against.

When Jesus was baptized and the Holy Spirit descended on Him the Bible says: "Immediately He was lead of [by] the Spirit into the wilderness to be tempted of the devil". It was the Holy Spirit picking the fight! That same Spirit is IN us and has no fear of the devil at all. The devil knows God has all power. Jesus said He gives US power to "Trample on snakes and scorpions and over ALL the power of the enemy". Romans 6:14; "Sin shall NOT have dominance over you" [anymore]. The devil is a spirit but sends his numerous human servants at us all the time. They are usually someone we love like family to bring us down. We should stop thinking everything coming against us is a real demon. It is usually just a foolish UNSAVED human doing evil. The demons cannot just come in and possess us. If they could they would control us all. We do need to stay away from his realm of witchcraft, séances, And Ouija boards etc.

With all these chapters on missing Heaven this one is about POWER and VICTORY. Jesus cast demons out a man so possessed he broke chains. Healed a man born blind and raised the dead. He even told the wind and waves to be still. He is the one who does our fighting. All we do is rest in His power. We know the "suffering of this present time is not to be compared to the GLORY that shall be in us". Jesus came down and experienced all that we went through and won with flying colors. "In all ways was tempted as we were". "There has no temptation befallen us, but such as is common to man". Our troubles seem like we are only ones, but we're not. Many went through and got the victory. Hebrews 11 tells of the Bible's hero's. Read what they went through and didn't even have a whole Bible to see the successes. Read how; "The world was not even worthy of them" [to even have such Godly people down here]. We do know all the victory songs in Churches we sing often. But we don't show victory in our lives. We concentrate on the END not the NOW! We keep our eyes on the prize! We know the devil already lost this war. If we don't let our love for any human distract us we can win. That's why Jesus said: "If we love any more than Him we can NOT be HIS disciple". The devil will come at us with those we love the most. "A man's foes shall be they of his OWN household".

There will be no excuse for not making this journey. All we need to win we have been given. It's us who make God look bad when we are weak and fearful. We put Christ to an "Open shame" when we show weakness to the world. Revelation 21:8 speaking of those who went to the Lake of Fire, before it mentions any SINS it says; "The fearful". It is a sin for Christian to be fearful. We that are strong are to help the weaker ones who don't study the Bible to get the faith they need and are following false Preaching. "The angels rejoice more over one that repents than 99 who need no repentance". We saw how many went through the Great Trib. And missed Heaven in Rev. 7:9. I am doing all I can to reach as many as I can to save them from that fate. Rev, 14:4 speaking of the 144,000; "These are they who follows the Lamb where so ever He goes". Not the 2 billion professed Christians who claim Him. That 144,000 will multiply to 200 million once the 144,000 and 2 Witnesses soon start Preaching. That's where this title comes from "1 billion 800 million". Rev. 9; "200 thousand, thousand"; DON"T MISS Heaven!

CHAPTER 22

"VICTORIES IN POETRY"

I wanted to show a few poems I wrote when I first came back to Lord 19 years ago. There were 13 poems, and they just came at unexpected times in their entirety. They show the VICTORIES I got. I was a Junkie, Alcoholic, Criminal, and Mental Patient for 31 years and the Lord changed me from in one day without any human treatment programs.

"Drinker or Drunk"

Do you drink and not bathe, and smell like a skunk?
You don't do it on purpose, I know I was a drunk*
Do you drink the good stuff, and buy no junk?
To me it didn't matter, because I was a drunk*
Never used a chaser I was a man, not no punk;
My throat burned like hell. Not a thing to a drunk*
Cheap wine I loved dearly, I never faked the funk;
Night train 20/20 not a wino, a drunk*
Drugs I liked also, good dope not no bunk;
Still my greatest love was to go and get drunk*
They said; go to Church fool, do something be a monk;
But in all those temples, there's no way to get drunk*
Then Jesus from Heaven saw the level I had sunk;
Bound the demon of liquor, His grace saved this drunk*

"Junkie's Only"

When I first stuck a needle into my veins;
The high was so good, pure peace and no pain*
They called me junkie, but I did not care;
When I cooked up my dope, with no one I'd share*
The rush oh the rush, when you first run it in;
Was so beautiful and lovely, darn if it was a sin*
I shot heroin cocaine, Ritalin and speed;
It soon changed from pleasure, to a no joking NEED*
As my veins started collapsing, I shot in my neck;
If you don't believe that, look closer and check*
Cadillacs we called them, police call them tracks;
Those needles left long trials, with no way to get back*
They said go to treatment, but drug programs failed;
The Law had a sure cure, 10-20 years in jail*
Some junkies did beat it, when I asked they'd boast;
They'd found the best shot was the Holy Ghost*
I tried it, it worked, before my life I did lose;
Here's the way out Junkie, what will you chose*

"Christian Happiness"

I float on a cloud, but not in my dreams;
All through the day to no one I'm mean*
I'm happy I'm smiling yes it's been this way;
For nearly 6 months, I believe it will stay*
My Joy and my peace, I cannot explain;
But one thing I know, I can't be insane*
I do good to others, I pray day and night;
Deep in my soul there shines a bright light*
Christ put it in there, when I asked Him in;
Now no more am I, a weak slave to sin*
I'm now Heaven bound, and I never frown;
What I want now, is to tell the whole town*

That this joy I feel, it stays it's for real;
If they want it too, their heart Christ will seal*
When time comes to an end, and they need a friend;
They sure will need one when judgment begins*
In the book of life my name will be;
And Christ will be there, to speak up for me*
No more will I worry of hell or of death;
Because while on this earth, His words I have kept*
If you start to pray and ask Him today;
He'll come in your heart, and there He will stay*
We'll go to a place not made with hands;
And listen to music from an all angel band*
We'll be there forever, where it's day never night;
It's all because, we saw and came to the LIGHT*

"CHRISTMAS CAME EARLY"

Did you get a present for Christmas this year?
One that brought joy, peace happiness and cheer*
Was your present so good it thrilled your soul?
And will you cherish it, as if it were gold*
So where will you keep it, this gift you love dear?
It must be kept safe, to last through the year*
You don't want it broken, or faded or lost;
It has so much value, you can't put a cost*
I got a present just like that this year;
And I don't want to lose it, it's always kept near*
My gift did not come on Christmas you see;
It came in July that was Christmas for me*
That love joy and peace you get in December;
I got all that too and will always remember*
The gift I received, I had only to believe;
That Christmas means Jesus, now both are in ME*

There are 9 others, but I just wanted to give you a few. Feel free to use them, just don't sell them. I have the copyrights.

CHAPTER 23

"THIS ISN'T NEW"

All things in this book are not new. Most Christians have been in Churches decades, and just read right over them. It's time to take a second look before the judgment. God kept some thing's to be revealed in the last days and most are in Revelation. But even the parables are a mystery to most. Most all the parables have a last day reference. Most have to do with thee "Judgment Seat of Christ" that Churches never preach about. Why? Maybe they don't want to scare away the members? Maybe they don't want to lose the money from the offerings? Maybe they just don't understand them? Whatever it is you need to know whether they preach it or not it WILL happen. When we go up we are not going straight to Heaven. We all have a stop to make at His Judgment to be checked. They are plainly in the parables if you re-read them with this in mind. Every time Jesus said "cast them", He was doing it from the CLOUDS, not the earth.

We all have things we keep secret in our life. Some of those are willful sins that only God knows. He will reject us at Judgment if we don't change and repent [turn from them] now! We can have the whole church fooled but not Him. Christians seem to think we are supposed to blessed all the time. Jesus gives a parable of a servant doing the things he is supposed to do comes in and expects to be fed by the Master. Jesus no; "you feed ME first". We get paid when our jobs are done, not before. We are supposed to be on a job. Our reward comes at the end.

Christians want it now and then. Praise and worship means nothing if we are not doing our first job first!

This "Forsake All" should be easy to understand if we look at it like the love of a mate. Look how your mind day and night are on that one you love? Look how you do anything to please that person. Look at how the love songs stress the extremes people go through for that person. If we loved Jesus that much he would always be on our minds like David said; "In that Law does he meditate day and night". No mate would let you get away with seeing and thinking of them one day a week. If we really believed in Heaven we would send our treasures up there. But we stock pile treasures down here. "Where your treasure is there will your heart be also". All know about the mark of the beast. Do they see "when" he makes the law that? "No man can buy or sell without the mark", it covers everything they have? They will lose everything anyway so why even get them? You will see your real heart is really with your treasures! You won't give up your earthly possessions. You will think if God was real He would have come back by then like the preachers said. And you LOST your FAITH!

This book is written because most all assumed Heaven was in the bag. Not even Pastors preach about the New Earth, because they can't explain who goes there for real. They don't tell the difference hell and Lake of Fire because they don't understand that either. There's too much they don't know to put your eternal life in their hands. Jesus wants to deal with YOU! Rev. 3:20; "If any man [singular] open, I will come to him [singular], and sup with him [singular] and he [singular] with ME". I tell my class all the time; "They only need me until THEY learn to hear the leading of the Spirit themselves. Then they don't need me anymore. With their separate ministry MORE will be saved. These Pastors want to keep you ignorant to keep your money and their seats FULL! The Spirit is in you all. Learn to hear His leading from your own thoughts.

So to be clear on what will happen to the 1 billion 800 million is they will inherit the New Earth after the Great Tribulation, or Hell on earth for the living. They believed and were baptized so as Jesus said they get eternal life. BUT WHERE; is up to us? We cannot receive the same reward as the one who forsook all. Those who trusted in denominations will see they are what Rev. Calls; "Clusters of the Vine of the Earth". If Jesus is the true VINE [Religion] these others are the Religions of MEN! There is only one Church and all who accepted Christ names are in His book. He hopes those in Him will get it right before Judgment. Because there, He MUST reject those who accepted Him, but followed someone else! You cannot be His disciple, and you won't be with Him in the City of Gold [Heaven]. All the preaching and witnessing done these religions DO bring people into salvation. It puts them in the safety zone from the Lake of Fire. Now they can only go to HELL if they don't get it right. I know this seems new but it's not if you put as much effort into understanding the Bible as you do others things you love.

Let's look again at John 3:16. "Whosoever believes in Me shall not "PERISH". And other places it says; "Not condemned". Perish and condemn mean the Lake of Fire, never to be heard from again! That's the first thing we are saved from, the Lake. The second thing the Great Trib. And Wrath of God; 1 Thess. 1:10 & Ro. 5:9. We are supposed to be saved from that Wrath IF we hear and obey Christ, not the denominations [bundles and clusters]. Christ needs no middle man to Him. Most all are following the "Traditions of the Elders" not Christ. He warned of the MANY fakes who would come, yet most don't take time to check. The wheat and tares will be separated at Judgment. It was the enemy that put the tares in Christ's field. That's him in Rev [angel with power over fire] 14:18 saying to the other angel with the sharp sickle; "Gather the clusters of the vine of the earth" [and send them BACK down here to ME! It's the devil who KNEW Jesus could not accept your false beliefs. He gets a second chance to get you to get his MARK. You will be starving and thirsty but the mark is the only way you will get any food. You will have to die to get the New Earth in a slow horrible way. You've seen the pictures of holocaust Jews when the allies entered the camps? Skin and bones they were! Get it right this first time and you won't have to deal with that 2nd part of the Trib. "He that will seek to save his life SHALL lose it" [in that 2nd Trib.]

Getting saved is just part 1. We can sit back and wait on Heaven if we want. Or we can do like the man who found treasure in the field. He bought the whole field! The man who found the pearl of great price, sold all he had to buy it. Both sold all. Jesus said the Kingdom of Heaven was like both these people. If we love Jesus like these loved the treasure and pearl we would sell out also. But we got too much to do of our own business. The Lazy Servant who hid the Lord's money wasn't sitting idle all the years the Master was gone. He was doing something! He was doing his own thing, and making gain for himself. He put Gods work aside, not his own.

I have NO goals in life but to do His will. I'm not seeking to buy anything. I really believe and this world is not my home. He has work that needs to be done, and most don't have time. If you don't have time for Him, don't expect to go His Heaven. He's coming for His ELECT. His best! All the "Lukewarm" [average, casual and mediocre] will not be chosen. He didn't say you weren't saved; just you were AVERAGE. And you will MISS Heaven!

"SUMMARY"

This book was not meant to hurt or shame anyone. It was meant to help those who truly love God but just don't understand scriptures very well right now. They know some things they are hearing from the pulpit don't seem right. It is you who this book is for. I have relatives who will never change from what they were taught. "You can't put new wine in old bottles". Did we receive the Word as a LITTLE child? Are we open to be taught that we may have received bad information?

Here's how critical it really is. I wrote a study; "3 Strakes you're Out". It comes from Rev 14:9-11. It shows who burns forever in the Lake, and who doesn't. We were taught people burn in hell forever; wrong! All must come out of hell at the 2nd resurrection Rev 20:13. The only humans who will be tormented forever with devil and his demons are those who; "Worship the beast, and his Image, and get his Mark". All other unsaved will receive the 2nd death eventually [after they pay for ALL their sins] in the Lake of Fire. That's why it called the 2nd death! BUT those who make Heaven didn't fall for any of it. You see the worship of the beast comes a year or so BEFORE the False Prophet comes in and makes the Image. Then tells all to get the Mark. 90% of Christians will worship that first beast [666 guy] thinking he's a good guy [Rev 13:8]. Not until the next beast starts mentioning the mark do they realize they were wrong. Now ALL those Christians WILL Miss Heaven. Rev 15:2 & 20:4 says; "They got the victory over the beast; Image and Mark". They didn't fall for any of the devils tricks. Everyone Going to Heaven heard Jesus voice, not the denominations! Even 1 strike you Miss Heaven!

Revelation 11:2 John is told to; Measure the Temple and Altar and them who worship therein". And to not measure those in the "courtyard outside the Temple". They will be trampled by the unsaved and devil 42 months. Notice it's the Gentiles [unsaved] who are doing this to a 3rd group of people. The ones IN the Temple won't be here. The ones cast back are those lukewarm, average, sin willful, lazy, and would not RE-check Christians. John is told to TELL the Church who is going to make it and who won't unless they repent. Yes John the disciple is one of the 2 Witnesses. If you don't believe me, at least believe him. He'll be here soon with Elijah and the 144,000.

Jesus said; "What I tell you in the ear; that shout ye from the housetops". I'm shouting what He gave me. It's not some secret either, it's been in the Bible 2,000 + years. John 7:7; "The world cannot hate you but Me it hates, because I testify [speak up] of it, that the deeds thereof are evil". No one wants to speak up and go against the majority. No one wants to be in the FEW. They want human support.

It's only hard to do Gods will if we try to have it both ways. Once we see there's no other way we will fully surrender to Him and do it His way. Did we surrender fully? And to who did we surrender to? Him or a denomination? Christians are in the right place already, and Jesus hopes you will get it right before Judgment.

I'm humble and say like Paul said in 1 cor. 9:27; "Even I can be a castaway". The number one thing God hates is PRIDE. I'm praying for you not to MISS Heaven.

Bro. Fred